MACRAMÉ

An Easy Beginners Guide to Macramé. All the Patterns, Techniques, and Secrets You Need to Know to Decorate Your Home and Garden Creatively. Including 60+ Handmade Projects

Written by:
Jade Paper

© **Copyright 2020 by Jade Paper — All Rights Reserved**

The content contained within this book may not be reproduced, duplicated, or transmitted without direct written permission from the author or the publisher.

Under no circumstances will any blame or legal responsibility be held against the publisher, or author, for any damages, reparation, or monetary loss due to the information contained within this book. Either directly or indirectly.

Legal Notice

This book is copyright protected. This book is only for personal use. You cannot amend, distribute, sell, use, quote, or paraphrase any part, or the content within this book, without the consent of the author or publisher.

Disclaimer Notice

Please note that the information contained within this document is for educational and entertainment purposes only. All effort has been executed to present accurate, up-to-date, and reliable, complete information. No warranties of any kind are declared or implied. Readers acknowledge that the author is not engaging in the rendering of legal, financial, medical, or professional advice. The content within this book has been derived from various sources. Please consult a licensed professional before attempting any techniques outlined in this book.

By reading this document, the reader agrees that under no circumstances is the author responsible for any losses, direct or indirect, which are incurred as a result of the use of the information contained within this document, including, but not limited to, errors, omissions, or inaccuracies.

Table of Contents

Introduction 6

CHAPTER 1: Macramé Knots That You Can Create 12

    Various Ways to Use Macramé Garden Plant Hangers 16

        Plants Plant Hanger 16

        How to DIY Macramé Plant Hangers? 17

    Health Benefits of Macramé Garden Plant Hangers 18

    Beautiful Craft of Macramé Garden Plant Hanger 20

CHAPTER 2: Easy Projects 22

    1. Folded Braid Keychain 22

    2. Macramé Necklace 23

    3. Heart Keychain 25

    4. Serenity Bracelet 42

    5. Celtic Choker 45

    6. Macramé Glass Connector Bracelet 54

    7. DIY Tassel and Macramé Keychains 56

CHAPTER 3: Intermediate Projects 57

    8. Macramé Wall Hanging 57

    9. A Macramé Inside Decoration 60

    10. Nautical Rope Necklace 63

    11. Macramé Fringe Tassel Pillow 65

12.	Double Coin Knot Cuff	69
13.	Prosperity Knot Belt	71
14.	Snake Knot Tie Backs	74
15.	Switchback Bracelet	77
16.	Barefoot Macramé Sandals	80
17.	Pet Leash	83
18.	7-Point Snowflake	86

CHAPTER 4: Advanced Macramé Projects 90

19.	Modern Macramé Hanging Planter	90
20.	Wreath of Nature	96
21.	Macramé Gem Necklace	105
22.	Macramé Skirt Hanger	108

CHAPTER 5: Macramé Projects 112

23.	Macramé Tote Bag	112
24.	Macramé Sunscreen Holder	115
25.	Mini Macramé Christmas Ornaments	117
26.	Mini Pumpkin Macramé Hanger	121
27.	Bohemian Macramé Mirror Wall Hanging	123

CHAPTER 6: Macramé Hanging Projects 126

28.	Door Hanging	126
29.	Circle Wall Hanging	129
30.	Boho Wall Hanging	132
31.	Adorable Pom-Pom Tassel Wall Hanging	135

CHAPTER 7: Macramé Home Decors 138

    32.   Chic DIY Plant Hanger 138

CHAPTER 8: Macramé Bracelets 140

    33.   Macramé Bracelet With Rattail Cord and Glass Beads . 140

    34.   Black and Red Macramé Bracelet 149

    35.   Fish Bone Macramé Bracelet 151

    36.   Side by Side Macramé Bracelet 153

    37.   Cross Choker 156

CHAPTER 9: Macramé Accessories 160

    38.   Yarn Twisted Necklace 160

    39.   Filigree Lacelet Bracelet 163

    40.   Designer Hat 170

CHAPTER 10: More Macramé Accessories 176

    41.   Hearty Paperclip Earrings 176

    42.   Fringe Fun Earrings 179

    43.   Lantern Bracelets 185

    44.   Hoop Earrings 193

CHAPTER 11: Macramé Home Décor Projects 196

    45.   Macramé Tie-Dye Necklace 196

    46.   Macramé Wall Art 199

    47.   Easy DIY Macramé Wall Hanging 205

CHAPTER 12: More Macramé Projects 212

48.	Amazing Macramé Curtain	212
49.	Macramé Charm and Feather Décor	216
50.	Hanging Macramé Vase	221

CHAPTER 13: Macramé Jewelry **233**

51.	Day Glow Earrings	233
52.	Macramé Spiral Earrings	237
53.	Summery Chevron Earrings	242
54.	Easy Macramé Ring	247
55.	Sun and Moon Anklet	250
56.	Macramé Rhinestone Ring	252
57.	Macramé Watch Strand	256
58.	Silky Purple Necklace	259
59.	Leathery Knotted Necklace	263
60.	Rhinestone Macramé Bracelet	267
61.	Intricate Lavender Macramé	271

Conclusion **275**

Introduction

The Art of Macramé

For men and women who would like to grasp how-to Macramé, there is a range of areas available on the marketplace. Creating intricate knots that produce whole patterns that could likewise be transformed into exquisite bracelets, flower baskets, and decorative wall-hangings is just what Macramé is based on, being an artist. The exact and elaborate first step in trying to understand how exactly to get into Macramé, in case you are interested in this topic, is to understand how basic knots work and a couple of diagrams.

Beginner Macramé

Just like anything in life, you will encounter an endless amount of techniques to start analyzing a new craft or art. I am not likely to claim an expert on Macramé. I am an entire newbie. From a newcomer into another, I will simply take you throughout my private journey to demonstrate one method to execute it.

I shall provide each of the instruments which you will need to find your solution to make the enjoyable art of Macramé. The good thing is you do not have to develop into a professional to create fantastic decoration bits for your dwelling. Frankly, it seems much more robust as it is. Thus, let us enter it.

First: Exercise precisely the ideal method to do Macramé

Why should the proceedings that you exercise cost? Like anything, that endeavor is precisely about to price you a tiny bit. Exactly how much?

My first "real" job cost me around $30 because of the Macramé rope (and sometimes even Macramé cord, since it may be understood) and a few dollars because of its very own wooden dowel.

Macramé Practice Job

Reasons why I urge a little "clinic" job:

It fills the time gap as you patiently wait for the Macramé rope.

This will allow you to get familiar with different Macramé knots, their titles, and the way to complete them.

By the conclusion of your clinic effort, you are going to be joyful and totally eager to go bigger, or you are getting to see this is not for you personally.

Completing this clinic effort will provide you precisely the assurance to commit your cash and time to choose the subsequent step into a first "real" Macramé undertaking.

Exactly What Macramé Job Can I Make?

Decide concerning precisely what job you may need to create. Look over pictures of Macramé on the Web. It is possible to hunt Etsy, Pinterest, along Google. Do some research to master everything that exactly is available at the marketplace.

What sorts of Macramé activities will I produce?

Start small:

- Plant holder.

- Jewelers such as choker necklaces or bracelets.
- Wall-hanging.
- Novel mark.
- Key string.

Bigger jobs comprise:

- Dining table.
- Hammock (rescue a significant job such as this).
- Lighting-fixture.
- Carpet.
- Headboard.
- Garland or bunting.

Choose the job type. Wall-hangings and plant Holders will most likely be both common new-comer tasks.

Where is it planning to move? This can help determine what dimensions you are attempting to produce.

Locate a design that suits you; longer free form and organic or symmetric with traces that can be fresh and readily defined patterns?

Where Can I locate Macramé Patterns?

Whenever you have determined what sort of job and design attracts you personally, you are all set to search for a design. I came across my regimen Etsy for under 5.

You do not need to get a design. You will find a gazillion YouTube pictures that could assist you through the construction of many tasks that you may possibly undoubtedly love. 3 main reasons I decided to get a blueprint would be:

- I had been searching through Etsy for suggestions for what kind of project I desired to produce and realized at the point that buying patterns was an alternative. I fell in love with work that has been precisely what I had been imaging.
- Patterns are an inexpensive choice ($5–$10).
- I enjoyed the idea of not having to work side by side, working with an image, stopping and starting it frequently. Getting off on my computer seemed more relaxing for me.

What Stuff Do You Need for Macramé?

Once you have your own project/pattern, you are going to know exactly how much rope to purchase. I presumed that I had to utilize an organic cotton collection. However, it is likely to let your personal taste and design show you as you choose your shade & stuff. They promote rope (or cable) around Etsy. But it had been inaccessible at the price or number I desired. Adhering to a great deal of hunting, this is the connection that I used.

Can I Achieve This?

Yes, I am here to let you know that you can.

Here is a very small behind the scenes confessional of my own experience:

How Often Could I Choose to Learn a Macramé Knot?

Inside my clinic endeavor, I lost track of the number of times I had to repeat the movie into the beginning and begin. And that I would have moments after I wondered whether that really been because of me personally. Because of this, it is entirely reasonable to have momentary doubts alongside your learning curve.

Selections to the Macramé Project

Under supplies, I recorded "rolling clothes stand" this is precisely what I used, and what I was advocated; however, it is costly and maybe not mandatory for those who never have one.

You can work together with your dowel or ring wrapped out of anywhere that is suitable.

You can hang it in a doorknob, a drawer, or even anyplace you will observe to secure your own piece.

Other thoughts would be to use a more suction cup hook or maybe an over-the-door wreath hanger.

You may Defeat a piece of artwork hanging out your walls (temporarily) and hold your bit by the nail.

Assessing outside a diagram, nevertheless well methodical and clarified that it will likely be, will not provide you plenty of assistance to allow you in order to do Macramé precisely. It is crucial to find a ribbon to have the capability of Macramé effectively. Like some other gained art, attempting to understand just how exactly to Macramé, in addition, calls for training. Obtain some clear, training samples of diagrams that are simple to secure started. You may quickly realize the ones that are simpler to make eventually become more uncomplicated compared to the intricacies of the ones that are elaborate. You will manage to progress for them with a great deal of exercise and time.

CHAPTER 1: Macramé Knots That You Can Create

You have to be questioning what does finding out about various Macramé knots have anything to do with pastimes. Well, come to believe of it, making multiple Macramé knots is absolutely nothing less than a hobby. Let's provide a bit more gratitude for this specific and gorgeous pastime and see what Macramé knots we can make. Easy techniques to tie Macramé knots? Go over the actions exposed listed below to reveal how easy it is, in fact, for making the knots. Browse for Macramé plant wall mount guidelines to discover out more.

1. **Square Macramé Knot**

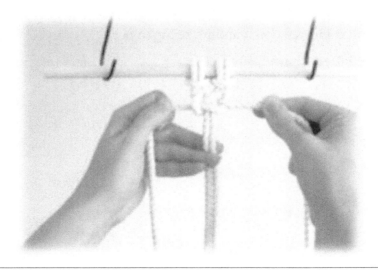

To make this knot, you'll need:

- 3 cables (red, orange, and green).
- 1 security pin.
- Cardboard.

Take all 3 cables in hand and connect a knot on the top to secure them together. Use a security pin to repair them on the cardboard.

Pull-on both orange and red cables in order to finish the knot. Bring this brand-new knot as close to the initial one we made.

Now get the red cable and bring it under the green cable. It goes over the orange cable. This makes a loop.

Then get the exact same orange cable and go below the red cable towards the left. Maintain the pattern of cables from delegated right red, green, and orange. Take the best orange cable and cross it over green cable.

In precisely, the very same way, repeat the actions to develop square knots for as long as you want the string to be.

2. **Plaited Chain Stitch**

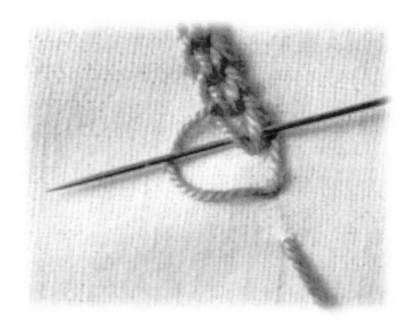

To make this Macramé knot, you'll require having:

- 4 cables (grey, purple, white, and pink).
- 1 security pin.
- Cardboard.

With a knot, you will have the ability to attach the cables together. Retain the pattern of cables from delegated right - pink, white, grey & purple. Go and take the grey cable over white and purple cables. Now proceed and take purple cable and discuss pink and white cables. Make a loop around both cables and pull it through.

Bring the grey cable down now and start the specific very same actions utilizing the pink cable now.

Create a loop around the 2 cables and pull it through. Go behind each of the 4 cables and bring the grey cable to the left side.

Take all 4 cables in hand and connect a knot on the top to protect them together. Utilize a security pin to repair them on the cardboard. Whit method you'll work your way down the cables and make Macramé knots bracelets or pendants.

3. **Vertical Lark's Head**

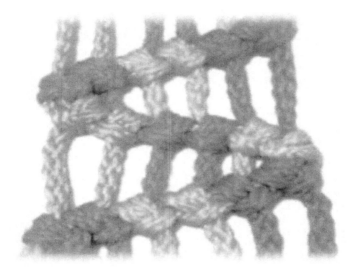

Another part of the look of the Macramé plant wall mount is the pot that you pick to have the plant in. There are so numerous various kinds of alternatives here, and you can experiment with the color of the pot and how it matches and blends with the color or the look of the plant, as well as the rope or cable that you hang it all together with.

Various Ways to Use Macramé Garden Plant Hangers

You can select a choice of plants that do well outdoors, and then make a series of plant wall mounts. You can make the plant wall mounts, and hang them someplace outside, like on a patio or terrace. There is a range of various patterns and designs you can knit the wall mount in, so it is possible to actually tailor the look of the wall mount by utilizing various patterns. Some are more ornamental than others, for instance, while others are easier and plainer, and have a more Spartan or practical look. Merely pick the pattern that can finest fit the space that the wall mount is positioned in and begin to knit away! Another excellent method to utilize Macramé plant wall mounts is in spaces that benefit significantly from the peace and charm that plants can offer. Bedrooms can frequently be brightened up by the addition of a plant, and it is truly charming when you have a good plant in your bedroom if you invest an excellent quantity of time in there.

Plants Plant Hanger

Individuals are starting to value the significance and advantage of having plants inside the house or office anywhere possible, and Macramé plant wall mounts can quickly be made DIY. If you select to create a Macramé plant wall mount by yourself, they can be made exceptionally inexpensively, too.

Macramé plant wall mounts are really not a brand-new thing. It likewise provides various methods to show plants than what individuals are generally utilized to, and you can see them from multiple angles than you would if they were kept on the ground or at a desk.

How to DIY Macramé Plant Hangers?

You can make the plant wall mount in a method that highlights the netting itself, by selecting a truly good rope or piece of string to put the plant and the pot in. You can likewise experiment with connecting various knots in the rope that you hang the plant and wall mount in to alter the look of the wall mount in general.

Many individuals select to knit their wall mount rather than merely utilizing rope or twine and connecting knots in it. This can be an enjoyable and more challenging variation of the job, and it is a fantastic thing to handle if you are a proficient knitter. It takes significantly longer to knit the wall mount rather than merely utilizing rope or twine, so ensure you have the time and energy to see such a task through before you take it on.

They are likewise great locations to have one or numerous plant wall mounts, as they can end up being a truly significant part of the space and enhance the landscapes from outside the conservatory, which is quickly noticeable thanks to the various windows and glass walls that they include. In an area like this, it is best to make a plant wall mount that is in light or soft colors, so that it does not subdue the surroundings from outside the observatory or the interior of the location.

To get this knot, you'll require:
- 2 cables (dark blue & white).
- 1 security pin.
- Cardboard.

Take both cables in one hand and connect a knot on top to protect them together. Utilize a security pin to repair them on the cardboard. In the underside, with the white cable, bypass the dark blue cable, then under it; take it up and over, and in the end, in the loop.

Always keep the pattern of cables from delegated right - dark & white blue.

Most of the work will be carried out by the white cable. Cover the white cable over the dark blue cable, fold it under, and then through the loop.

This pattern must be something comparable to: over, under, through and under, over, though. Eventually, all you require to do is duplicate the actions throughout the cables.

Health Benefits of Macramé Garden Plant Hangers

The craft was so popular in the seventies that practically everybody's decks would be embellished with Macramé wall mounts of numerous colors and utilizing various kinds of Macramé cables.

More plant wall mounts might be discovered to bring indoor plants in the living room and the cooking area, where large windows would open to the yard, letting the breeze in.

The Macramé plant wall mounts made terrific concepts for a craft task or for a handcrafted present for a good friend. The craft is so simple to do. It can be carried out only on one day and even half a day. Kids were taught to Macramé by their grannies, aunties, and mommies.

Having indoor plants helps get rid of approximately 96% of carbon monoxide gas from space every day, according to research studies performed by NASA.

Particular plants are understood to get rid of other harmful contaminants, such as formaldehyde from the air. This nasty toxic substance can be discovered in all sorts of unwary locations, such as a brand-new carpet, or artificial upholstery.

To begin with, plants produce needed oxygen; soak up toxic substances and CO_2; tidy up the VOCs released by plastics, carpet fibers, paint, and artificial structure products that trigger Sick Building syndrome, headaches, aching, dry throats, scratchy or dry skin, and tiredness; assist individuals in recuperating rapidly from an illness, and develop a calmer and more calming environment.

Making Macramé plant wall mounts, or offering one as a present, motivates growing indoor plants. What more thoughtful gift could you provide to like ones in your house than developing a healthy environment? And what much better method to present indoor plants into the house than with some upgraded, modern-day Macramé wall mounts?

Keep in mind, making Macramé plant wall mounts for your house or as presents, and it is not a secure plant wall mount. Keeping that in mind, it's time to get your Macramé cables and begin knotting!

The Flower Power generation had it right the very first time. There is a health advantage in surrounding your household with flowers and green plants. An excellent way to grow plants and flowers is to plant them in pots and to hang some utilizing Macramé plant wall mounts.

Precisely what can Macramé plant wall mounts provide for your health? As it ends up, indoor plants offer lots of health advantages, aside from being popular house designs.

Beautiful Craft of Macramé Garden Plant Hanger

This wall mount is a fantastic present which can be provided out to your liked ones. With Macramé plant wall mounts, you have the option of either keeping your plants inside your home or outdoors without any damage to the plants.

Macramé plant wall mount is amongst the different types of Macramé, which is restoring the attention it should have. Plant wall mounts are one of the most popular products in the gorgeous art of Macramé.

Macramé plant wall mount is suitable for revealing off your plants. You can put your potted plants in the wall mount to provide an incredible and natural appearance.

The different colors of the Macramé plant wall mount offer you the chance to choose the ones that fit your taste. If utilized as outside plant wall mounts, guarantee your color option matches the underlying tone of the structure.

The craft of the Macramé plant wall mount is taken by some individuals as a pastime. You have fewer products to utilize, for this reason, minimizes intricacies associated with some works.

Macramé plant wall mount is ending up being the style now. Macramé plant wall mount is a natural craft.

In conclusion, the lovely craft of the Macramé plant wall mount has actually come to remain. Let's utilize it to show our plants for a more natural touch in the house, work environment, gallery, and so on.

CHAPTER 2: Easy Projects

1. Folded Braid Keychain

Supplies
- Rope.
- Small elastic band.

Instructions
1. Cut 3 bits of rope somewhat more than twice the length you need for the completed custom keychain.
2. Stack them, even the strands, and wrap one end with a small elastic band a couple of inches from the ends.
3. Do a straightforward mesh. Stop when you are at the same distance from the closures as the elastic band is.
4. Circle one end through the keychain. If you'd like, put the elastic band around the 2 closures to hold them erect.
5. Tie knots in the sections of the bargains to wrap it up.

2. Macramé Necklace

Macramé has gotten uncontrollably mainstream over the last few years for its uniqueness, high quality, and tasteful look. Making Macramé yourself gives you an excellent opportunity to create unique pieces. Before we shared an instructional exercise for some lovely Macramé wall quality structures that you can add to your home or office style. Here we present to you an instructional exercise for a straightforward DIY Macramé necklace, ideal for matching with all of your midyear outfits!

Our DIY Macramé necklace uses a progression of the most fundamental Macramé knots: the square knot.

Supplies

- 1 chain and decorative discoveries. We found our copper chain at our nearby jewelry store and afterward used a lobster fastener with 2-hop rings. We used a copper key ring for our middle, yet don't hesitate to pick another sort of metal that better accommodates your style!
- While you're in your jewelry store, you can also choose small beads to fit into your Macramé weaving. Just make sure the beads are the same thickness as your string or the beads will fall off! The whiter material is a cotton cord, and the grayish material is a hemp cord. When your materials are ready, follow the step-by-step photographic training exercise below to pleat your DIY Macramé necklace.

3. Heart Keychain

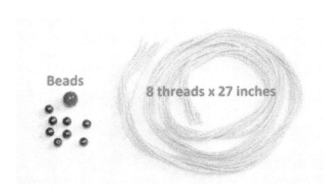

Beads

8 threads x 27 inches

Supplies

- 8 smaller beads.
- 1 big bead.
- 8 threads each 27-inch long.

Instructions

1. You will be making an overhand knot. Take 1 thread, fold it in half, now form a loop on top of the folded thread. This can be done by using your thumb as a guide to how long the loop should be. Then hold the thread at this length so that the loop is isolated.

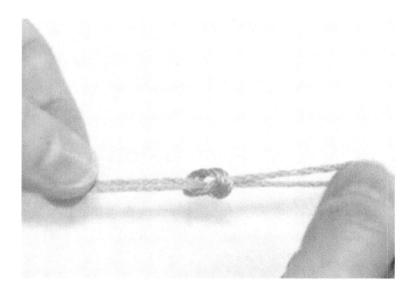

2. While keeping the loop isolated, create another loop with the rest of the thread and then place the original loop through the new loop while keeping hold of the original loop, and

then when through you can pull to tighten. You should end up with something like the picture below.

This is what your overhand knot should look like.
3. Take another one of your threads, place it over your previous thread with the knot in it ensuring that the knot is in the middle of the new thread you have just chosen.

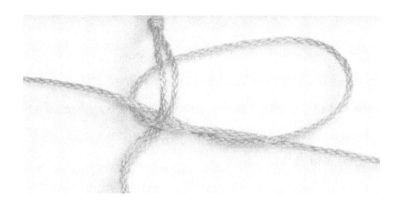

4. Now you are going to tie a square knot. Take the left-hand side of the thread that you have just lay down (the one without the knot) and place it over the thread above it and under the thread on the right. Then take the right-side thread and thread it under the thread at the bottom and under the left-hand side and through the loop that has been created by the left-hand thread. Simultaneously, pull the threads on the left and right side so that it tightens, and a knot is formed.

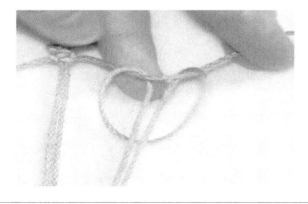

5. Take the single thread on the right, place it over the 2 threads in the middle and under the left thread. Now take the left thread under the 2 threads in the middle and under the loop created on the right. Pull to tighten (both sides at the same time) and create your knot.
6. Take the single thread on the left, and then take the single thread on the right. Ensure that both threads are horizontal. For now, you will only be working with the right so you can set the left side down until later.
7. Take a new single thread, fold it in half, and make sure there is a loop created at the top. Then place the thread behind the only thread on the right and fold over the top. Now, pull the 2 loose threads through the middle of the loop so that it looks as above. Then remove the threads so that the thread tightens, and you will end up with a lark's head knot.

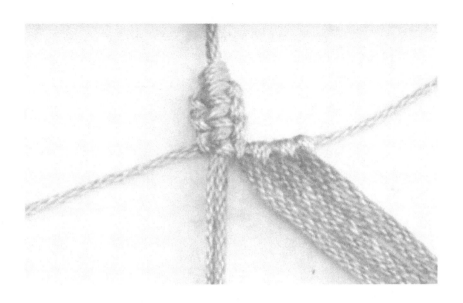

8. Take 2 more single threads and repeat step 7 until you end up with 2 more lark's head knots on the right.

9. Take the left single thread, which should be horizontal as stated earlier. Then create 3 more lark's head knots on the remaining single thread. It should look like the picture above.
10. Now you should have 3 lark's head knots on each side.
11. You should now have 2 threads in the middle. Take a small bead and thread it onto the 2 threads.
12. Take a big bead and place it on the same thread pushing it to the top so that your Macramé piece looks like the one in the picture.

13. Tie a simple overhand knot at the end of the middle thread, under the beads, so that the beads are locked in place. There are instructions above on how to do this.
14. Take a pair of scissors and cut the loose thread at the end of the knot leaving just the knot.

Refer to the image above.

15. From your left group of threads, take the first on the right and place it horizontally across the other threads in the bunch. Then take the thread next to it, loop it over the horizontal thread, under itself, then using the same thread loop it over the parallel thread again and finally through the loop created. Pull to secure the knot tightly. You will have a half-hitch knot.
16. Repeat this step with each thread until all threads on the left have been done.
17. Take the next thread, directly under the half-hitch knot, on the right. Pull this thread across horizontally and repeat the process of creating the half-hitch knot.

18. Repeat this process 6 more times so you have 8 half-hitch knots in total like the picture below (excluding the one at the bottom).

19. Here you will be creating the knot at the bottom of the left side.
20. Take the first thread on the right of the bottom knot. Then take the thread next to it, loop it over the horizontal thread, under itself, then using the same thread loop it over the horizontal thread again and finally through the loop created. Pull to secure the knot tightly. You will have a half-hitch knot.

21. Take the thread used to create the half-hitch knot and place it around both horizontal threads, under itself, then using the same threads loop them over the horizontal threads and finally through the loop created. Pull to tighten.

22. Then take the thread just used for the horizontal thread and place it across the remaining threads. You should have 3 horizontal threads. Take the threads next to it and wrap them around the 3 horizontal threads to create a half-hitch knot.

Take the next thread and wrap it around both horizontal threads, under itself, then using the same threads loop them over the horizontal threads and finally through the loop created. Pull to tighten

23. Repeat this process, add 1 thread each time, until you get to the last thread. Your Macramé piece should look like the image above.
24. This is what your finished left side should look like. If you have made any mistakes it is okay to go back and change them. The last half-hitch knot can be hard to follow but use the pictures to aid you and you will succeed.

25. For the completion of the right side, start in the same way you did for the left side. This is the same process and if you completed the left side you shouldn't find it too hard. Repeat the steps given previously.

26. When completed it should look like the illustration given above. Don't worry if you don't get it the first time. You can always undo your stitching and try again.

27. With the hanging threads from both the left and right sides, pull to make sure they are vertical. The threads should be together as one group.
28. Cut a piece of the thread, around 4-inch, and fold it in half to use. Now place this piece of thread in the middle of the bunch but sitting on top and the 2 ends facing the top as in the picture (purple thread).
29. Take a single thread from the group of threads. Wrap it around the group of threads as shown above.

30. Continue to wrap the thread around the group of threads until there is only a short portion of the single thread left. There should have been a loop created by the short piece of thread cut earlier (purple thread in photo). Place the end of the thread (purple) through the loop as shown, pull the 2 ends of the loose thread (purple) at the top so that the loose thread (purple) will come out ultimately. The end of the single thread becomes trapped inside the loop creating a knot.

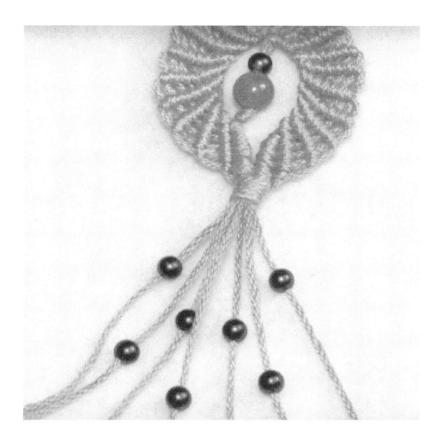

31. You should have several threads hanging loose from the knot just created. Place a small bead through each thread and show them to have the same intervals between them. They should be staggered creating the pattern shown.
32. Now do an overhand knot at the end of each bead to secure it in place. Refer to earlier instructions on how to complete this.
33. Trim the remaining threads from underneath the knots.

34. This is what your final Macramé piece should look like. You will have a beautiful keychain to use yourself or gift to someone.

4. Serenity Bracelet

Supplies

- White C-Lon cord, 6 ½ ft., x 3.
- 18 frosted Purple size 6 beads.
- 36 purple seed beads, size 11.
- 1 of 1 cm. purple and white focal bead.
- 26 dark purple size 6 beads.
- 1 of 5 mm. purple button closure bead.

Note: the button bead needs to be able to fit onto all 6 cords.

Instructions

1. Take all 3 cords and fold them in half. Find the center and place it on your work surface as shown.
2. We will now make a buttonhole closure. Just below the knot, take each outer cord and tie a flat knot (aka square knot). Continue tying flat knots until you have about 2 ½ cm.
3. Undo your overhand knot and place the ends together in a horseshoe shape.
4. We now have all 6 cords together. Think of the cords as numbered 1 through 6 from left to right. Cords 2 and 5 will stay in the middle as filler cords. Find cord 1 and 6 and use these to tie flat knots around the filler cords. (Note: now you can pass your button bead through the opening to ensure a good fit. Add or subtract flat knots as needed to create a snug fit. This size should be fine for a 5 mm. bead). Continue to tie flat knots until you have 4 cm. worth. (To increase bracelet

length, add more flat knots here and the equal amount in step 10).
5. Separate cords 1-4-1. Find the center 2 cords. Thread a size 6 frosted purple bead onto them, then tie a flat knot with cords 2 and 5.
6. We will now work with cords 1 and 6. With cord 1, thread on 1 seed bead, 1 dark purple size 6 beads, and 1 seed bead. Repeat with cord 6, and then separate the cords into 3 and 3. Tie a flat knot with the left 3 cords. Tie a flat knot with the right 3 cords.

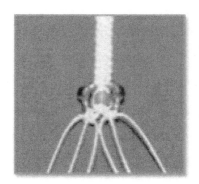

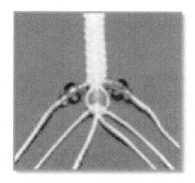

7. Repeat steps 4 and 5: 3 times.
8. Find the center 2 cords, hold together and thread on the 1 cm. focal bead. Take the next cords out (2 and 5) and bead as follows: 2 sizes 6 dark purple beads, 1 frosted purple bead, and 2 dark purple beads. Find cords 1 and 6 and bead as follows: 2 frosted purple beads, 1 seed bead, 1 dark purple bead, 1 seed bead, 2 frosted purple beads.
9. With cords 2 and 5, tie a flat knot around the center 2 cords. Place the center 4 cords together and tie a flat knot around them with outer cords 1 and 6.
10. Repeat steps 4 and 5 4 times.
11. Repeat step 3.
12. Place your button bead on all 6 cords and tie an overhand knot tight against the bead. Glue well and trim the cords.

5. Celtic Choker

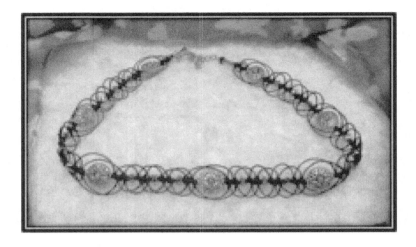

Elegant loops allow the emerald and silver beads to stand out, making this a striking piece. The finished length is 12-inch. Be sure to use the ribbon clasp which gives multiple length options to the closure.

Supplies
- 3 strands of black C-Lon cord; 2 7 ft. cords, 1 4 ft. cord.
- 18 green beads (4 mm.).
- 7 round silver beads (10 mm.).
- Fasteners: Ribbon Clasps, silver.
- Glue Beacon 527 multi-use.

Note: Bead size can vary slightly. Just be sure all beads you choose will slide onto 2 cords.

Instructions

1. **Optional:** Find the center of your cord and attach it to the top of the ribbon clasp with a lark's head knot. I found it easier to thread the loose ends through and pull them down until my loop was near the opening, then push the cords through the loop. Repeat with the 2 remaining strands, putting the 4-ft. cord in the center. If this is problematic, you could cut all the cords to 7 ft. and not worry about placement. (If you really trust your glue, you can skip this step by gluing the cords into the clasp and going from there).

2. Lay all cords into the ribbon clasp. Add a generous dap of glue and use pliers to close the clasp.

3. You now have 6 cords to work with. Find the 4 ft. cords and place them in the center. They will be the holding (or filler) cords throughout.

4. Begin your alternating lark's head (ALTERNATIVE LARK'S HEAD) chain, using the outmost right cord then the outermost left cord. Follow with the other right cord, then the last left cord. For this first set, the pattern will be hard to see. You may need to tug gently on the cords to get a little slack in them.

5. Now slide a silver bead onto the center 2 cords.

49

6. The outer cords are now staggered on your holding cords. Continue with the ALTERNATIVE LARK'S HEAD chain by knotting with the upper right cord.

7. Then tie a knot with the upper left cord.

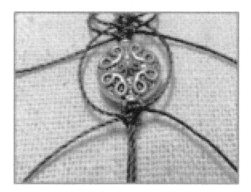

8. Finish your set of 4 knots, and then add a green bead.

9. Tie 4 ALTERNATIVE LARK'S HEAD knots followed by a green bead until you have 3 green beads in the pattern. Then tie one more set of 4 alternative lark's head knots.

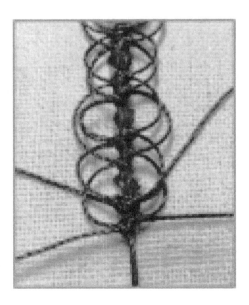

10. Slide on a silver bead and continue creating sequences of 3 green, 1 silver (always with 4 ALTERNATIVE LARK'S HEAD knots between each). End with the 7th silver bead and 1 more set of 4 ALTERNATIVE LARK'S HEAD knots, for a 12-inch necklace. (Use this to shorten or lengthen as you choose).

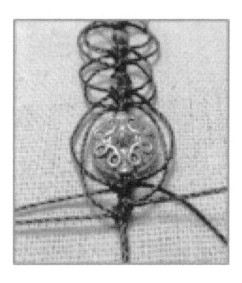

11. Lay all cords in the ribbon clasp and glue well.

12. Crimp shut and let dry completely. Trim off excess of the cord.

6. Macramé Glass Connector Bracelet

Supplies

- 3 m. of glass connectors and cords for each bracelet. I chose the 2 mm. string, but you can use 1 mm. (although I strongly suggest it should be 1,5 mm. longer at least).

Instructions

1. Take a 20 cm. piece and slip it over the connector leg.
2. Take the 1 m piece and tie your knot middle. You have 2 lines now, 1 to the left and 1 to the right.
3. Take the right string and slide it into the middle string and into the left string.
4. Take the left thread; slip it on the center string, then close the knot under the left string.

5. Repeat the steps until on one side you make the bracelet. Finally cut off those ends and then burn them to melt and stick and make the other leg. When you tie the knots, a spiral is formed. It's going to feel like that.
6. Switch to the second form now. Steps 1, 2, 3 are the same for this method as the first step.
7. The difference is that you don't repeat the same move repeatedly! After tying the first leg, slip the left cord under the cords in the center and over the right cord over the center and left cords.
8. Tie the knot, which looks like 2 knots.
9. Alternately tie the ties on either hand until the desired length is reached. Repeat the other side of the bracelet.
10. Change your bracelets with another short cord and the second option instead of a clasp. Combine both ends and tie the knots on both ends.

7. DIY Tassel and Macramé Keychains

Organize yourself by making a special keyring for all those small rewards cards. Use this to improve your Macramé skills. In order for the stripped Macramé keychain, I used vertical clove hitch knots and wool-roving thread. The third and fifth personalized keychains are super easy—strings and a few Perlis with a tassel. And the fourth DIY keychain is only a long braid, folded in half, wrapped in floss of embroidery. Beads are hand-painted and made from Scullery.

Supplies

- Keyring.
- 3/16-inch natural cotton piping cord.
- Beads.
- Embroidery yarn or floss.
- Scissors.

You can make things fancy on your Keychains tassel or Macramé by wrapping them in different yarn or floss colors.

CHAPTER 3: Intermediate Projects

8. Macramé Wall Hanging

Supplies

- Macramé rope. I have been using this 4 mm. rope, 12–16-inch cords are required (12). Note that this is a thick hanging wall, which is why we would need a longer cord. To act as your hanger, you would need a 1 shorter piece of cording. Simply tie it on either end with a simple knot.
- A dowel or a stick. I used a long (ha-ha) knitting needle. As long as it is straight and robust and as long as you need to work with what you have!

Instructions

1. The first thing you want to do with each end is to knot a cord. For our project, this will serve as the hanger. Making a Macramé wall hanging when it's hanging is much easier than lying flat. This can be hanged from cabinet knobs, doorknobs, a wreath hanger, or even a hanger for a picture. Just make sure it is robust!
2. Begin by folding in half your 16' cords. Make sure that the ends are the same. Place the cord loop under the dowel and thread through the loop to the ends of the rope. Pull closely. That's the Head Knot of your first reverse lark's. (For

assistance, refer to basic Macramé knots). Repeat with the other 11 cords.

3. First, make 2 square knots rows. Now make 2 rows of Square Knots Alternating. Now make 2 more Square knots sets. Follow this pattern until you have 10 rows in total (2 rows of square knots, 2 rows of alternative square knots). Working from left to right, make 2 half-hitch knots across your piece in a diagonal pattern. Now, from right to left—make double half-hitch knots across your piece in a diagonal pattern.

4. Have 4 rows in all. Make 2 more rows of square knots. We will finish the hanging wall with a set of spiral knots—This is basically a half-square node sequence (or left-side square branch). (Do not end on the right side of the knot, just make square knots and spiral on the left side for you again and again.)

5. To build this spiral, I made a total of 13 half square knots. Finally- I trimmed in a straight line the bottom cords. The total size for the hanging of my wall is 6.5" wide by 34.

9. A Macramé Inside Decoration

A Macramé inside decoration is a simple DIY venture that will add a high-quality touch to any room in your home. This free instructional exercise will assist you with making a tapestry with a lot of intriguing examples, for example, spirals and triangles. Try not to be reluctant to switch things up to make it your own. In spite of what it looks like, this is a basic undertaking that will simply take you 1–2 hours to finish. It truly meets up quickly and you'll discover loads of chances to add your own style to it. This is only one of many free Macramé designs that incorporate plant holders, bookmarks, shades, and a ton more. The bunches you'll be utilizing for this Macramé inside decoration incorporate lark's head tie, spiral bunch, and square bunch. You can figure out how to tie every one of these bunches by perusing our guide on the best way to Macramé.

Supplies

- Macramé line.
- Scissors. I'm utilizing a cotton clothesline for my Macramé line. It has a magnificent normal look to it and is genuinely reasonable.
- 1 wooden dowel on a table. The wooden dowel shouldn't be these careful measurements and instead of the wood dowel, utilize whatever size you like as long as you can fit all the ropes over it. If you'd prefer to give it a progressively outdoorsy feel, you could utilize a tree limb about a similar size.

- Cotton Macramé Cord (200 feet or 61 m.).
- Wooden Dowel (¾-inch measurement, 24-inch in length).

Instructions
1. Make a hanger for your wooden dowel. A Macramé rope connected to a wooden dowel with scissors adjacent to it
2. Cut a bit of Macramé rope that is 3 feet (1 m.). Tie each finish of the string to the different sides of the wooden dowel.
3. You'll utilize this to hang your Macramé venture when it's done. I like to connect it toward the start so I can attach the Macramé venture as I tie ties. Working along these lines is a lot simpler than laying it down.
4. Macramé line cut into pieces with a couple of scissors cut your Macramé line into 12 lengths of rope that is 15 feet (4.5 m.) long.
5. This may appear to be a great deal of line yet hitches take up more rope than you would suspect. It is highly unlikely to make your rope longer if you have to, so it's smarter to cut more than you'll utilize.
6. Warbler's head hitch on a wooden dowel. Crease one of the Macramé strings into equal parts and utilize a warbler's head bunch to append it to the wooden dowel.
7. Join the various strings similarly.

8. Bunch spiral stitches. A Macramé winding joins. Take the initial 4 ropes and make a left-confronting winding join (additionally called a half bunch sinnet) by tying 13 half bunches.
9. Keep knotting spiral stitches. 6 winding lines. Utilize the following arrangement of 4 ropes to make another winding fasten with 13 half bunches.
10. Keep working in groups with 4 lines. At the point when you finish, you ought to have an aggregate of 6 winding fastens.
11. Make square knots, a lot of square bunches. Measure roughly 2 creeps down from the last bunch in the winding fasten. This is the place you're going to put your next bunch, the square bunch.
12. Utilizing the initial 4 ropes, make a correct confronting square bunch. Keep making the correct confronting square bunches right over this line.
13. Give a valiant effort to keep them all on a level plane even with one another. You'll wind up with a lot of 6 square bunches.

10. Nautical Rope Necklace

Supplies

- Pendant with jump ring or bail.
- Ruler.
- Scissors.
- White nylon cord.
- Knotting board.

Instructions

1. Cut 7 feet or 84-inch of nylon cord.
2. Then, keep the strands together as a group. Tie an overhand knot around the 2 strings. Make sure there's 1–2-inch of space between them.
3. Make an overhand knot 6-inch away from the end. Tighten the knot by pulling individual strands and make sure to secure it on the knotting board. Separate the strands into 2 groups.
4. Take the left part of the cord and cross it under the right corner of the cord.
5. Get the right cord group and cross it over the left side. Tighten as you pull down and knot until you reach 16-inch.
6. Check the last double chain and make an overhand knot. Tie them 6-inch from what you have created. Add a pendant, if you want, and make sure you knot before and after adding it to keep it secure.

11. Macramé Fringe Tassel Pillow

Supplies

- Plain cloth zipper pillow cover in the components of your pillow inserts.
- A combination of enriching fringe trim (I discovered mine at yard sales, however, you can find some comparable here or there).
- Measuring stick.
- Texture scissors.

- Launderable texture pen.
- Texture glue (I used Liquid Stitch).
- Brawl check.

Instructions

1. I spread out my plain pillow cover. I most likely could have pressed it first; however, I'm not excessively that kind of young lady. At that point, I cut my first line of fringe trim to be the specific width of the pillowcase. No estimating fundamentals! Simply line it up and cut!
2. Spread out and cut the remainder of your columns of trim to length, and invest some energy adjusting them till you get them exactly how you need them on the completed item!
3. Make little checks on the edges of where your line of paste will be, that way when you flush out the fringe trim, you can use your measuring stick (or anything with a straight edge) to draw an obvious conclusion and make a straight line over with your texture stamping pen (or then again, if you're like me, you can use your child's Crayola marker since it's advantageously inside arms reach and it will be covered by fringe at any rate).

Fringe pillow instructional exercise:

1. Make sure to follow all the instructions on your texture stick (I used Liquid Stitch) and press out an even bit of glue across one of your pen lines.

2. At that point start toward one side and carefully push down the fringe trim as you go. It's alright if it doesn't go down high since you have a chance to straighten it out before the glue dries.

   Note: Of course, you can use a sewing machine rather than a texture stick for this, however, I simply would not like to upset attempting to control the pillow cover so that I wasn't sewing through the 2 layers. You may be a more skilled needleworker than me, however, so put it all on the line!

3. Stay back and ensure it's straight and in any event, changing as essential. At that point stick down the remainder of your columns in a similar way! Rehash these means on the other side of your cover so they reflect one another. Also, use the Fray Check on the edges to keep your trim from fraying!

4. This texture stick dries to the touch very quickly; however, I gave it a decent 24 hours before I upset it as a sanity check. I actually made 2 of these at a time, since I needed to take a stab at destroying one of them just to see how things were made! The primary time I've used Rit Dye was on this undertaking, so I'm a sorry ace and was somewhat threatened that I would destroy it. Be that as it may, I think it turned out really great! (The color I used was blue-green).

5. If I had let it soak longer, I'm speculating the fringe would have gotten darker and been nearer to a similar color as the cloth, yet I wouldn't fret this monochromatic looks great as

well! In case you intend to color yours, I suggest passing on the fringe and pillow cover independently before you fasten the fringe trim to the pillow.

Decoration fringe Macramé DIY pillow covers:

1. I left the other characteristic greyish material color since that is the look; I'm going for with our bedding circumstances!
2. The large cushioned white pillows are ones that I re-covered using a fleecy carpet some time ago, and I got the rich rosette pillows here (despite the fact that as the climate has chilled off, so it would be so comfortable to have these thick sewn pillows).
3. Anyway! The Boho Bedroom makeover with this instructional exercise for Fringe Tassel Pillow DIY, sat the point when I was amidst working on these pillows, *An Attractive Mess* blog posted about a shower drapery makeover using a comparative technique with the fringe.

12. Double Coin Knot Cuff

Double coin knots are usually tied in precisely the same way, one after the other, but the knots lie flatter if the knot's start is reversed, starting at the left, then at the right, and so on. This produces an enticing pattern of long strands looping around the top and bottom edges of the cuff, alternating between the double coin knots.

Supplies
- 9 m. (10 yds.) 2 mm. leather cord.
- 3 x 9 mm. internal dimension end caps magnetic fastening.

Instructions
1. Cut the leather cord into 3 equal pieces, 3 m (3 1/3 yd.) long. Referring to Chinese knots: double coin knot, tie a double coin knot using all 3 strands starting in your left-hand with a clockwise loop and pulling down the working end (right-hand tail) over the thread, complete the knot and make it tight, so that the top loop is relatively broad and all 3 strands are smooth and neatly aligned.
2. Make a second double coin knot, this time starting with a loop in your right hand, bringing the working end (left-hand tail) down through the loop, around the other tail, and doubling back to create the second knot.
3. Firm the second knot, adjust the position so that the previous knot is relatively close but does not overlap. Make sure none of the cords are twisted and that they all lie flat inside the knot.

4. Continue to tie double coin knots one by one, and swap the starting position from side to side each time.
5. Analyze the length of the cuff until you've made 6 knots. If required, adjust the distance between each knot to allow for the fastening.
6. Overlap the cords after the final knot to create a circle. Either tie the cords together or stitch them across to hold the cord flat, depending on the style of your end cap (see Finishing Techniques). Trim the ends and use epoxy resin glue to hold them into the end caps.

13. Prosperity Knot Belt

The knot of prosperity is a broad flat knot in the form of a rectangle, which makes it ideal for belting. You can tie only 2 knots one by one, but inserting a double coin knot in between holds the belt flatter, allowing you to change it with the buckle to a more precise length. You might attach beads between the knots to embellish or hang charms from 1 or 2 loops.

Supplies

- 8.5 m (9 yds.) 2 mm. wax cotton cord.
- 12 mm. (½-inch) long buckle.
- Small piece of leather.
- E6000 jewelry glue.

Instructions

1. Fold the cord in half to locate the center and tie a double coin knot in the middle, beginning with a loop on the left side, referring to Chinese knots: Prosperity knot, a somewhat loose knot of prosperity tends to tie in, firm by raising all of the overlapping cords up, one at a time, to the top of the knot, until 2 loops are left at the bottom.
2. Pull through the top left cord to pull one side of the bottom loop up. Repeat on the other side. Then pull the tails one by one to get the knot tight.

3. Repeat the firming up the process if necessary to create a 12 mm. (1/2-inch) wide, closely woven prosperity knot. Hold the knot tightly in 2 hands between fingers and thumbs, and agitate gently to align the cords in a pattern that is even more woven.
4. Tie a double coin knot to the tails, this time starting with a loop on the right side. If the knot is tied, change the location, so it is similar to the knot of success but does not overlap it. Carefully set it up because you won't be able to change it later.
5. Continue to tie alternative stability and double coin knots.
6. Remember to alternate the side on which the start loop is an on-left loop for the prosperity knot and the right loop for the double coin knot.
7. Stop after tying a prosperity knot once the belt has the appropriate length allowing for overlap. Loop the ends twice on either side around the belt buckle to fill the void, and stitch tightly backward.
8. Cut a 1 x 3 cm. (1/8 x 11/8-inch) leather strap to create the belt loop.

9. Apply glue to one end of the leather strip and hold below the buckle over the stitched cord ends. Loop the strap around the belt, so it overlaps on the opposite side, leaving a loop wide enough to pass through the other end of the belt. Apply glue to the overlapping strip and stay until the adhesive seals. Leave before use, for 24 hours.

14. Snake Knot Tie Backs

These directions are for a tie back measuring approximately 40 cm. (16-inch) long, but the length can be easily adjusted: require 1,25 m (50-inch) of elastic cord for every 10 cm. (4-inch) of finished braid. You may leave the braid plain or adorn it with beads. Given that the elastic cord is very rigid and hard to thread through when inserting the beads, it is much simpler to use a tapestry needle to create a route for the finer needle.

Supplies

- 5 m (51/2 yd.) 3 mm. teal elastic cord.

Swarovski elements:

- XILION beads 5328, 4 mm. pacific opal and chrysolite opal, 54 each.
- Seed beads 11 (2.2 mm.) blue marbled aqua and silver-lined crystal.
- Nylon beading thread.
- Size 10 beading needle.
- Tapestry needle.
- 2 end caps with 3 x 9 mm. internal dimension.
- Epoxy resin adhesive.

Instructions

1. Cut a 45 cm. (18-inch) length of Knotted Braids: snake knot, work the braid on your snake knot.

2. Tie a knot to a beading thread at the end of a nylon length (or equivalent color) and thread 10 beading needle. Bend the braid from the end about 5 cm. (2-inch), so you can see the pattern of the cord between the loops on one side. Place the needle of a tapestry between the 2 straight braid lengths you can see.
3. Move the needle of the tapestry through the braid to escape between the loops on the other side. Leave the needle in place for the tapestry; this is the direction the finer threaded needle takes through the braid.
4. Hold the nylon thread between 2 lateral loops above the needle. Pick 1 aqua seed bead, 1 pacific opal XILION, 1 aqua seed bead, 1 silver seed bead, 1 chrysolite opal XILION, 1 silver seed bead, 1 aqua seed bead, 1 pacific opal XILION, and 1 aqua seed bead.
5. Place the beads through the braid at an angle, then take the beading needle back alongside the tapestry needle. Remove all needles simultaneously.
6. Pull the thread taut over the braid to protect the beads. Between the next loops thread the tapestry needle again through the braid, in order to attach another line of beads. This time the XILIONS order is inverted, adding 2 opal chrysolite and 1 opal pacific.
7. Repeat to add bead lines, stopping from the end of the braid about 5 cm. (2-inch) apart. Sew firmly in ends of thread.

8. Cut the cord to the same length, leaving the tails approximately 2 cm. (3/4-inch) long. Mix a bit of epoxy resin adhesive and put a cocktail stick within one end cap. Place 2 of the cord ends in the end cap and force the remaining cord in place using a cocktail stick (or awl). At the other end, repeat to add an end cap, and leave to dry.

15. Switchback Bracelet

This bracelet is not a fixed pattern and can be made with various knotting techniques in your combination. Work about 51 cm. (20-inch) to wrap around your wrist 3 times, and check the positioning of the beads on the bracelet as you go as they should be on top of your wrist instead of below.

Supplies
- 1.25 m (1½ yd.) 1 mm. off-white pearlized leather cord.

- 3 m (3 1/4 yd.) per 1 mm. and 1.5 mm. brown wax cotton cord.
- 5 m (5 1/2 yd.) SuperlonTM Tex 400 (0.9 mm.).

Swarovski elements:

- Square Mini-beads, 8 6 mm. light silk.
- Double Delica (size 8) seed beads, approx. 50 dark topaz rainbow 103.
- Metal button.
- E6000 jewelry glue or epoxy resin adhesive.
- Pin boa.

Instructions

1. To avoid damage to the pearlized leather, use the lark's head knot to loop a short piece of scrap cord around it, and attach it to a pinboard or work surface.
2. Using the 1.5 mm. wax cotton cord and referring to the Switchback braids: single cord Switchback braid, continue working 8 cm. (3-inch) of standard switchback braid over the leather thread. After approximately 2.5 cm. (1-inch), adjust the loop size to suit the button you use for the bracelet, and then continue.
3. Pick 14 double delicacies on each end of the leather chain. Drop 1 of the wax cotton cord's tails and work the stitched switchback (see Switchback Braids: Stitched Switchback Strap) by pressing beads between the knots, locking them as you tie the next knot together.

4. Move to the SuperlonTM Tex cream and function a standard switchback duration of 8 cm. (3-inch). Work the first half of a square knot in Macramé (see *Macramé: Macramé Knots*). Take a square mini-perch on 1 string, and feed the other tail in the opposite direction through the opening.
5. Tie a square knot to both cords of leather, so that the bead lies flat. Add 7 more mini-beads, after each tie a square knot. Perform another 2.5 cm. (1-inch) of the creamed switchback.
6. Continue to work the second half of the bracelet using various cord thicknesses, going from normal switchback to stitched switchback, double delicate beads, or working lengths without beads if you like. Finish worked with the 1 mm. wax cord with a length of the standard switchback.
7. Test the weight, then tie the button to the end of the leather cord; trim the leather, and use epoxy resin or E6000 jewelry glue to adhere to the reverse side of the button.

16. Barefoot Macramé Sandals

Supplies

- Pure cotton yarn or Macramé cord.
- Scissors.
- Large hole beads, for instance, the silver spacer beads.
- The Bulldog clips.

Instructions

1. Make 3 pieces of yarn or cords about 3m long then locate the middle point of the strips and make a knot. It's essential that the yarn is long; it will be needed for the ankle straps.

2. On one of the sides of the knot, braid strands of 2–3-inch together.
3. Loose the knot which was earlier made, and tie it again once you've made a spiral loop along with the braided strand. This creates what is called a toe loop of your sandal!
4. 4.The major sandal part, which goes down from the ankle, to cross the foot's front and then towards the toe, generally, is made using square knots. There are half a dozen strands to use now, so, divide them into 3 strands, with each having 2 strands.
5. From the right side, put that strand on top of the one in the middle, making a D-shaped looking loop. The strand located on the left should be threaded underneath the one in the middle and inside the loop with D-shape.
6. To make or create the leading section of the square knot, pull the right and the left strands. In the opposite direction, do the same thing for the left side. Move the strand on the left side over the one in the center, and then thread the strand on the right-hand side under the one in the center and backwards into the D-shaped loop. Draw the strands on the right and on the left from the one in the middle to finish the first square knot.

7. Make 2 other square knots, in addition to the first square knots tied. Next, thread the round beads made of silver on the strand in the center. Then around this same bead, begin the initial part of the next square knot.
8. Repeat steps 6 and 7, there should be a total of 10 beads, which would be joined to the center strand with a Macramé square knot (a few more beads are needed for bigger sizes).
9. Complete the section with beads by making 1–2 plain square knots that have no heads and separate the strands in 2 with each split have about 3 heads. Braid the strands to form the straps for the ankle, till a length/diameter of about 50 cm. is reached. This will allow you to wrap them around your ankles a few times. Alternatively, another bead made of silver can be added towards the end between a square knot for some decoration.
10. When doing this, it is essential to make 2 knots (double knots) towards the bottom part of the final square knot to make it firm. Cut off any remaining unused thread and repeat the steps above to make the sandal's second leg.

17. Pet Leash

Supplies

- Swivel Hook.
- Glue.
- 4 mm. or 6 mm. cord material.
- Project board and pins.

Note: The length of the material (leash) after the work is done should be determined by you and after you have selected it, you should try out this calculation: Length of the leash (in inches) = WC (WC)/3 (in yards).

The length of the holding cord also increases by 0.5-yard for every 10-inch the length of the leash is, beginning from 20-inch which is 2-yard long (i.e., 20-inch = 2-yard, 30-inch = 2.5-yard, 40-inch = 3-yard, and so on) till you get to your desired leach's length.

The total amount of materials needed is, therefore dependent on this calculation.

Instructions

1. Put the 2 cords vertically on our board after getting their corresponding midpoints and tightly place them close to one another. The longer WC should be on the left because that is what will be used to tie the larks head knot on the holding cord.
2. Half of the vertical lark's head knot should be made to move using the WC over or under (as the case may be) the holding cord to have a counter-clockwise loop. Gradually pulling it left, you should make it go over the WC to get the crossing point. Once the crossing point is reached, tie the other half of the vertical lark's head knot by passing the WC under or over the holding cord, while pulling it left, pass it under the WC also to make the crossing point.
3. More vertical larks head knot should be tied and should be done from the center in the direction of one end. When the first half of the handle is 6-inch, you should stop.

4. The whole sennit or cords should be rotated and back to the center, leaving the WC on the right. Loops should be made in clockwise directions as tying of Knots is resumed, and once the handle attains a length of 12-inch, you should stop
5. The 4 segments should be brought together, thereby folding the sennit. Locate the WC in the process. Tie a square knot using the 2 WC, and it should be tight. The fillers are going to be the short cords.
6. Folding the 2 WC means we should have 4 cords to work with. A suitable decorative knot by the user should be used alongside this beautiful design, some of the best knots to use alongside it are the square knot, the vertical larks head, and the half-hitches with holding cords. A minimum of 6-inch material should be attached to the hook at the end of the pet leach.
7. To attach the hook, 2 cords should be passed through the loop that is on the hook, and a tight finishing should be tied with the 4 cords. The usage of glue comes in here as the 4 cords are being tightened, the glue should be used. When it gets dry, all additional materials should be removed or cut to make the work very neat and beautiful. You may also consider another finishing style which entails that you move the ends in the direction of the strap and put it under the back of the knots so that it can be very firm.

18. 7-Point Snowflake

Supplies

- 1 1.5-inch ring.
- Any household clear drying glue or fabric.
- 2 mm. or 14-yard white cord material.
- Project board and pins.

Instructions

1. All the cords should be mounted to the 1.5-inch ring with LHK. It can be done by folding the cord and placing it under the ring, then brings the 2 ends over the front of the ring and down. The ends should be passed over the folded area. A reverse half-hitch should also be tied, passing the ends under and over the ring and under the cord. All the other cords should go through this step, and at the end of this step; the cords should be organized into a group of 7 having 4 cords. All the knots should be well tightened so that it won't loosen later on.
2. 2 square knots should be tied with each group of 4 cords. The fillers should also be pulled to tighten them firmly; this ensures that the first rest against the knots that are on the ring.
3. The 4 cords from the 2 square knots should be numbered. The cords should be alternated by using cords 3–4 from a square knot and using cords 1–2 from the other square knot. At this juncture, one must be careful in selecting the 4 cords that come from the 2 adjacent knots while tying the alternating square knot in a circle or ring.
4. The other cords should also follow after step 3 in order to complete the second row.

5. The cords should be alternated again so that the same group is used as is done in step 2. The third row of the alternating square knot should be tied all the way around the 7-point snowflake. Ensure that the knots in this row are a ½-inch beneath the knots from the second row.
6. I'm sure some novices may be wondering when the 7-point being talked about will take shape. Well, the designs will come alive soon. A picot has been made beneath on every one of the knots of step 5 using the 4 cords we just did. Now, let's get back to business. A square knot should be tied below one of the knots that were tied in row 3.
7. We need to make sure the knot rests against the one tied in step 5 above, so we move the knot up allowing it to form 2 picot loops
8. Still, with those same 4 cords, we will tie another square knot that is close to the one that was recently tied. Before tightening the knots, glue should be applied to the fillers. Once the glue gets dried, the ends should be trimmed to 1-inch, and a fringe should be formed by separating the fibers at the ends of the 7-point snowflake
9. Steps 6 to 8 should be repeated with another set of cords

10. There is a higher percentage that the knots may loosen as time goes on if a cotton cable cord is being used, and although this is an optional step, it is also advised. The snowflake can be turned over, and fabric glue should be applied behind each knot. Another thing to take note of about the fabric glue to be used is that it must be such that it dries clear.

CHAPTER 4: Advanced Macramé Projects

19. Modern Macramé Hanging Planter

Plant hangers are lovely because they give your house or garden the feel of airy, natural space. This one is perfect for condominiums or small apartments—and for those with minimalist, modern themes!

Supplies
- Plant.

- Pot.
- Scissors.
- 50 ft. Paracord (parachute cord).
- 16 to 20 mm. wooden beads.

Instructions

1. First, fold in half 4 strands of the cord and then loop so you could form a knot.

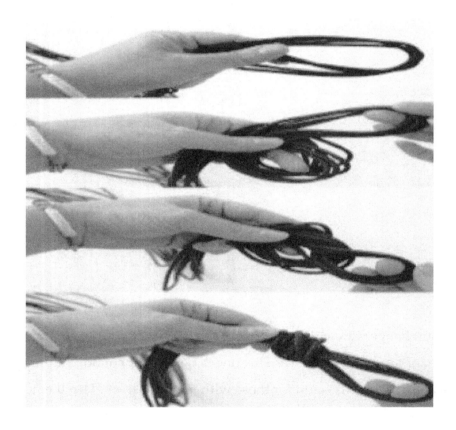

2. Now, divide the cords into groups of 2 and make sure to string 2 cords through one of the wooden beads you have on hand. String some more beads—at least 4 on each set of 2 grouped cords.

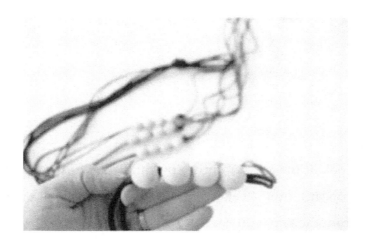

3. Then, measure every 27.5-inch and tie a knot at that point and repeat this process for every set of cords.

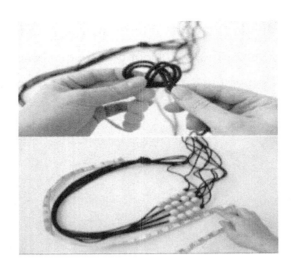

4. Look at the left set of the cord and tie it to the right string. Repeat on the 4 sets so that you could make at least 3-inch from the knot you have previously made.

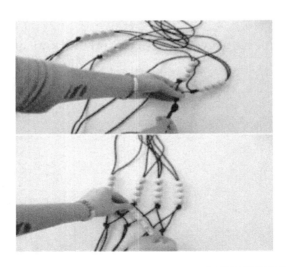

5. Tie another 4 knots from the knot that you have made. Make them at least 4.5-inch each.

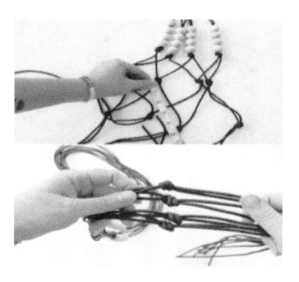

6. Group all of the cords together and tie a knot to finish the planter. You'll get something like the one shown below — and you could just add your very own planter to it!

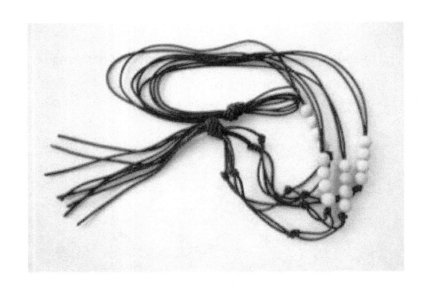

20. Wreath of Nature

Just imagine having a Macramé wreath in your home! This one is inspired by nature and is one of the most creative things you could do with your time!

Supplies

- Clips or tape.
- Fabric glue.
- Wreath or ring frame.

- 80-yard 12-inch cords.
- 160-yard 17–18-inch cords.
- 140-yard 14–16-inch cords.
- 120-yard 12–13-inch cords.

Instructions

1. Mount the cords on top of the wreath and make the crown knot by folding one of the cords in half. Let the cords pass through the ring and then fold a knot and make sure to place it in front of the ring. Let the loops go over the ring and pull them your way so they could pass the area that has been folded.

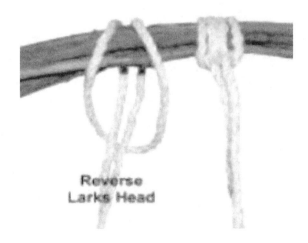

2. Let the ends pass over the first loop so you could make way for some half-hitches. Let them go over and under the ring, and then tightly pull it over the cord. This way, you'd get something like the one below. Repeat these first few steps until you have mounted all the cords on top of the ring. Organize them in groups of 10.

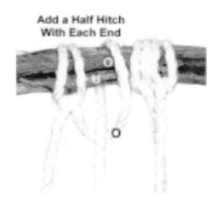

3. Now, you can make leaf-like patterns. To do this, make sure to number the first group of cords on the right side and make half-hitches in a counterclockwise direction. Take note that you have to place the holding plate horizontally. If you see that it has curved slightly, make sure to reposition it and then attach cords labeled 5 to 7. Move it to resemble a diagonal position and then attach cords 8 to 10.

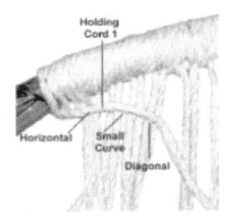

4. Make sure knots have been pushed close together and then use the cord on the left-most corner to lower the leaf-like portion. The first 4 cords should be together on the handle and then go and attach cords labeled 3 to 6 to the holding cord. Move the cords so they'd be in a horizontal position.

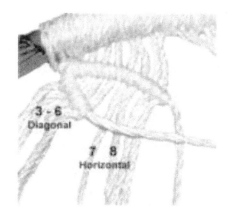

5. Now, move the cord upwards so that the center would not curve unnecessarily. Repeat the process for the cords on the bottom part of the frame and then start making the branches by selecting 2 to 4 cords from each of the leaves. Don't select the first and second row's first and last leaves.

6. Hold the cords with tape or clips as you move them towards the back of the design and decide how you want to separate—or keep the branches together.
7. Secure the cords with glue after moving them to the back.
8. Wrap the right cords around the ones on the left so that branches could be joined together.
9. Make sure to use half-hitches to wrap this portion and then use a set of 2 cords to create a branch.

10. Let the branches intertwine by checking the plan that you have written earlier and then use half-hitches again to connect the branches together.
11. Together with your wrap, make use of another wrap and make sure they all come together as one.

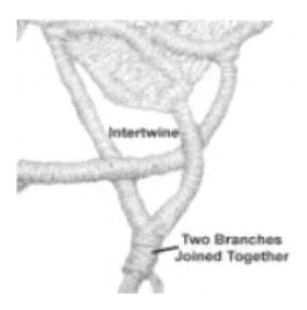

12. Secure the bundle by wrapping a 3-inch wrap cord around it and then let it go over the completed knot.

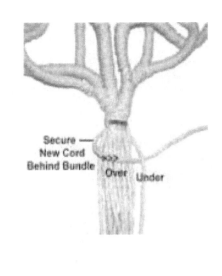

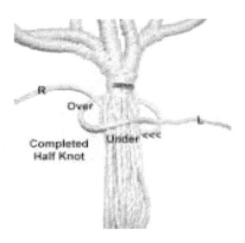

13. As for the fringe, you have to divide the knots into groups of 2 and make sure to tie a half-hitch on the right-most cord on the left, and then let them alternate back and forth continuously under you have managed to cover your whole

wreath. Let each sennit slide under the entire wreath and then attach each cord to the ring itself.

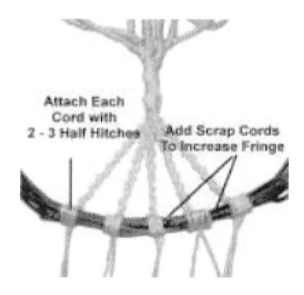

14. Make sure to divide the cords into small groups and then use the cords so you could tie the overhand knots. Unravel the fibers so you could form a wavy fringe.
15. That's it! You now have your own Macramé Wreath of Nature!

21. Macramé Gem Necklace

Supplies

- Gemstones of your choice.
- Beads.
- Crocheted or waxed cotton.
- Water.
- Glue.

Instructions

1. Get 4 equal lengths of cotton — this depends on how long you want the necklace to be.

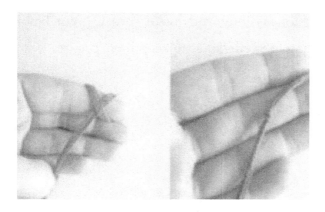

2. Tie a base knot as you hold the 4 cotton lengths. Once you do this, you'd notice that you'd have 8 pieces of cotton lengths with you. What you should do is separate them into 2, and tie a knot in each of those pairs before you start knotting with the square knot.

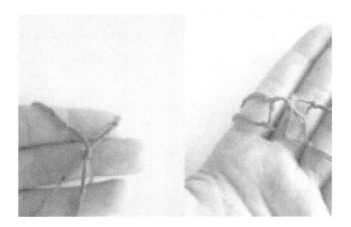

3. Tie individual strands of the cotton to the length next to it. Make sure you see some depth before stringing any

gemstones along and make sure to knot before and after adding the gemstones to keep them secure.

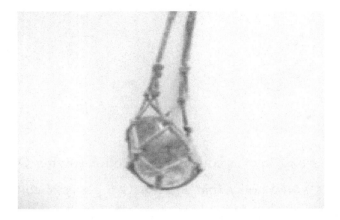

4. Take 4 of the strands in your hand and tie a knot on the top side of the bag. Tie strands until you reach the length and look you want.
5. Knot the ends to avoid spooling, and use water with glue to keep it more secure.

22. Macramé Skirt Hanger

Well, it's not really a skirt hanger. But it's something that could spruce up your closet or your walls.

It gives the room that dainty, airy feeling.

You could also use it for plant pots that are at least 8-inch in size.

Supplies
- 12 mm. size beads.

- 1 8-inch ring.
- 1 2-inch ring.
- 4 mm. cord

Instructions

1. First, cut 8 cords that are at least 8.5-yard long then cut a cord that's 36-inch long before cutting 4-yard of the cord.
2. Then, fold the 8.5-yard in half to start the top of the thread. Let it pass through the ring and let some parts drape down before choosing 2 cords from outside the bundle. Make sure to match the ends and then try the square knot.
3. To bundle the locks, you should find the center and move 8-inch down from it and then stop when you reach 12-inch.

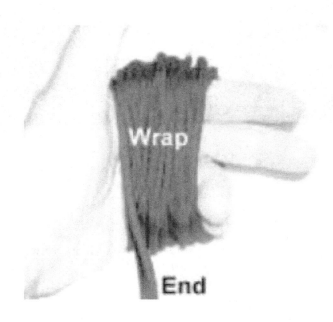

4. Wrap the center a couple of times and then pull the ends tightly until you build a sturdy bundle, and then tug on the ends so that the roll could get smaller.

5. Make a total of 4 spirals that could at least be 20-inch and then manage the filler cords by adding a bead to them.
6. To make the basket, attach the cords to the 8-inch ring by using double half-hitch stitches and then arrange the cords so they could be in 4 groups. Pull the stitches tightly so there's enough spacing and then mount all of the cords to the ring in a counterclockwise motion. To cover the ring, make sure to tie a half-hitch at each end.

7. Then, make alternating square knots just below the ring and divide into 2 groups of 40 strings each—it sounds like a lot but it's what would naturally happen. Add some tape to the cords you have labeled 1 to 40 and then tie a half-square knot to the 4 injected threads. Add some beads, and then tie a knot again.
8. Add beads to cords 20 to 21 after using cords 19 to 22 and then make alternating square knots and then repeat on the cords on the backside. Add beads and make more alternating square knots, then add beads to cords 16 to 17 after using cords labeled 15 to 18. Tie the row without adding any beads and then use cords 11 to 30. Work on cords 12 to 29 by adding beads to them and making use of alternating square knots. Repeat the 3rd row with no beads, and the 4th row with beads, and choose 4 of your favorite cords to make fringes.
9. Speaking of fringes, number the remaining cords mentally and then add a succession of 2 to 3 beads for each layer (i.e., 2/4/6 or 3/6/9) and then trim all the cords evenly.
10. Enjoy your new Skirt Hanger!

CHAPTER 5: Macramé Projects

23. Macramé Tote Bag

Instructions

1. Cut 10 ropes 2.3 m. wide. Fold half and fill the middle of the folded handle with the void. Take the ends of the rope and cross the last step of the loop you made. Pull close. Pull strong. Continue to attach 5 pieces of cord to each bag handle.
2. Separate 2 rope bits at one end and move the remaining rope to the other. We'll make the first knot with these 2 parts. Turn the left corner in the right corner and make a curve. Take the left (still straight) rope and fill the room with the 2 ropes you made. Remove the 2 corners until the knot is rising and in the right place. You want the handle to be approximately 5 cm. Take the left-hand rope and this time put it right to complete the knot. This time, thread through the gap the right side rope. Bring the knot tight again.
3. Create 4 more knots in a row on the handle with the rest of the ropes. Then continue again, but the first rope is missing this time, and the second and third ones tie. Continue along the route. You make 4 knots this time and you don't knot the first or the last rope.
4. When the second row is done, make the third row the same as the first (5 knots without missing ropes).
5. Upon completing the third section, repeat steps 2–4-inch the second handle. After that, bring the 2 handles face to face together.

6. Take both end ropes from the front of the bag and back to begin the next row. Fasten the ties on the front and back on the other end. You are then faced with the last lines on the front and back. Tie them together.
7. Knead until the strands are approximately 10 cm. left of the rope.
8. Cut the length of the rope 4 m. Use the same technique to tie it to the last knot of the handle.
9. Take the front and back strand and wrap the cord around. Place a double hitch knot and take 2 additional knots, one on the front and the other on the back.
10. Taking off the hanging rope. Link these strands instead of knots. You should apply some glue to cover them. Put it together to make a sheet.

24. Macramé Sunscreen Holder

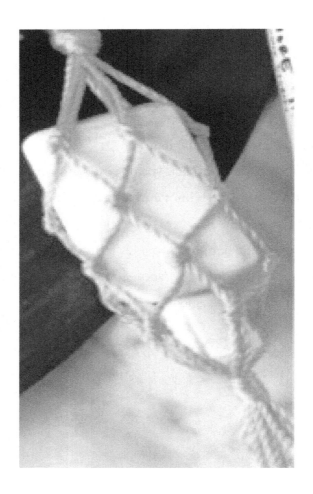

Supplies

- Line.
- Carabiner Cer.

- Sunscreen.
- A large empty bottle.
- Manager.
- Scissors.
- Candle.

Instructions
1. Cut 5 pieces of string about 20 cm. long.
2. Fold one big knit in half and tie it in the middle. Type the knot down to keep it.
3. Group the string into 5 pairs and each pair into 1" knot. Take another 1" down and tie the next set line.
4. Use this for about 4 rows of knots or span the length of your bottle. Glide into your bottle to test the fitness and number of knots required. I put the bottle down on the cap side for easy use.
5. Once the fit is correct, tie a big knot to hold the bottle with the strands.
6. Place each chord over the heat to melt the ends of the candle to prevent sprays.
7. Add a carabiner to your knot and add it to your curtain.

25. Mini Macramé Christmas Ornaments

Supplies

- Macramé cord.
- Harnesses.
- Blueberry or peanut.
- Masking tape.
- Scissors.

- Get the twig cords.

Instructions

1. Cut a little twig in the beginning and use the lark's knot to tie 6 cords to the end.
2. I wear cabinets, but before I added them to the twig I unwounded them and changed them from 3 to 1. Each cord should be about 2 m. long.
3. To tie a knot of a lark's, first, fold it halfway and lie down over the top of the twig in the center.
4. Bend the loop over the back of the twig and pull both ends up. Pull close.
5. Pull strong all 6 cords.
6. Repeat.
7. The first chain, which is 3 square knots, must be started once the strings are on the twig. These knots are connected to 4 cords so that the first 4 cords begin to be divided on the left.
8. To make the square knot, pull out the left cord to look like a "4" number.
9. Then tuck under the fourth string at the end of the first string.
10. So pick up the end of the 4th cord and pick the gap between the first and second cord that looks like the 4.
11. Tighten the 1st and 4th thread ends and move the nudge to the tip. It's the first half of a square knot.

12. You will do the same thing for the second half of the square knot but in the other direction. You form the 4 cords with the first and fourth cords but with the 4 cords on the right side.
13. Take the fourth first string. Then feed into the 2nd and third strings the 1st string tail and into the 4th shape through the opening.
14. Tighten the first and fourth thread ends, and you've got the first square knot.
15. Make 4 pieces of cord working. Keep another square knot and another square knot in the top row.
16. For the second section, you can only make 2 square knots. The first is divided into cords to do this. The second knot in row 2 will be followed by the next 4 cords. On the other hand, the other 2 cords are still left.
17. Use the 4-string center of a row just to form a square knot for the third row.
18. You can change the stress, try to keep your knots twisted and evenly spaced. 4 or 5 rows of small knot Macramé, taped to a table.
19. Repeat row 2 for row 4 with 2 square knots, leaving both cords at the ends.
20. Repeat row 1 for row 5 with 3 knots square.
21. Line 6-half hook knot. Take the first string and move the part horizontally to the half knot. It will be your lead thread.

22. Take the second cord from behind the lead and through the hole you made. Now make the same knot again with the same 2nd thread. This is half a jump.
23. Continue through the rest of the strings so that the lead cord is pulled through the other cords horizontally and directly. To save the knots, push the lead thread. Finishing of the decoration.
24. Cut the ends directly into a "V" down or up on the base to complete.
25. Then wear a hairbrush or a comb to brush the cord and build the fringe edge. Once you smooth it off, you can have to change the shape a little.
26. Cut the twig ends, then add a piece of string to hang the ornament up.
27. The second mini Macramé decoration I created for Christmas was the diagonal half-hitch. The half-hitch on the first is similar, just on a diagonal.

26. Mini Pumpkin Macramé Hanger

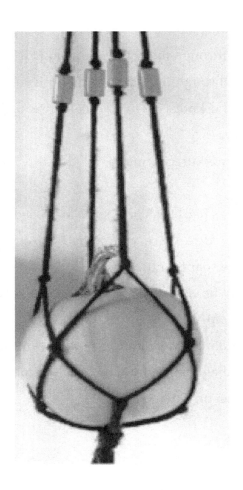

Supplies

- Black thread or line.
- Metal loop.
- Hollow pearls.
- Scissors.

Instructions

1. Cut 4 yarn strands about 3 times the completed hanger length. Fold the threads in the middle of the metal hoop.
2. The yarn strands are then divided into 2 groups.
3. Connect a knot to each group.
4. Cord a wooden bead on each thread, then tie another knot just below the bead.
5. Join a pair of knots a couple of inches apart.
6. Then tie 2 neighboring strings together and repeats each string. Then tie with the first line the last line.
7. Continue this process and bring another string together.
8. Finally, tie all the strings in a large knot.

27. Bohemian Macramé Mirror Wall Hanging

Supplies

- Macramé cord, 4 mm.
- Octagon mirror.
- 2 rings of wood.

- Wood Beads, size hole 25 mm. w/10 mm.
- Sharp scissors.
- Macramé mirror model.

Instructions

1. Cut 4 bits of Macramé into 108-inch (or 3-yard).
2. **Macramé lark's mirror knot.** Bend the strips in half and tie all 4 of them on the wooden cord with a lark's head knot. Tighten the ties and lock them. Divide the 2 lark's head knots into a square knot.
3. **Square knot Macramé mirror model.** Tie together 2 knots. Begin to tie 2 cubic knots into the second 2 lark's head knots.
4. **Mirror Macramé knot square.** When the second knot is started, bend it to one side of the other 2 knots to merge it into a big knot. Tie 7 knots square running on each side and on all sides.
5. **Macramé square knot creator.** After the knots are joined, break the ends. 2 strings on both hands and 4 strings in the middle. Place the string on the ends to show the broken ends. This makes it easier to add the beads. Thanks! It is the most challenging part! The rest connects only basic knots and even gets on the sides.
6. **Add Macramé perforations.** Place one bead on both hands. Place a knot on both sides under the bead to hold it even. Tie 4 strings in the middle or about 1/14 cm. below the beads.

7. **Macramé mirror beaded, Macramé mirror, white Macramé mirror simple knotted.** Take a single cord from the middle and attach it to the 2 cords on the ends. Bind the 3 on both sides in a knot. Connect the mirror even to the knot lengths. Attach 1 of the 3 side cords to the mirror back to keep it steady. Easy knots in all 3 cords at the left and right bottom of the mirror. Separate the 3 cords again. Put 1 on both sides of the mirror to place 2 on the front of the mirror and tie in a knot.
8. **Knots on Macramé mirror back, basic mirror Macramé technology.**
9. Flip the mirror over and tie all the cords together. Flip the mirror over and loosen the front knot. Glide into the knot at the back cords and straighten the knot. Cut the cord to around 14-inch. Pull the ends or loosen the strings and let the ends go. Combine a smooth comb with the ends of the thread. Hang and go!

CHAPTER 6: Macramé Hanging Projects

28. Door Hanging

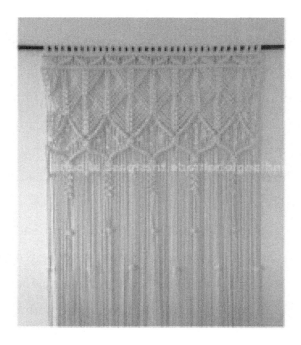

Supplies

- 25 long pieces of cords. The cords should be so long that they should be of the same measurement as your door, even when folded into 2.
- 1 wooden pole.
- Macramé board.
- Scissors.

Instructions

1. To get started, arrange the cords on your Macramé board and entwine them to the wooden pole using the lark's head knotting method.
2. The number of cords you should entwine to the pole should be 24. Do make sure the measurement of the ropes is of equal sizes even after they were entwined to the pole. Now, count out the first 12 cords, divide them into 2 equal parts, to have 6 cords on each side.
3. From the middle, take out 2 cords from each side of the halves and make a square knitting pattern with them. Take the foremost 2 from the left half and make a double half-hitch knot with the cords and then, continue with diagonal half-hitch knots until you are done with the half.
4. Make a double half-hitch knot with the 2 cords nearest to this patterned half, continue with the diagonal half-hitch knotting pattern until the second half becomes like the first one.

5. The distances you leave in-between the knots should be even, so that your work will look good. At this point, take 6 cords from the middle of the work and make a square knot with them. From the left rear, pick the first 2 cords, make a double half-hitch knot with them and go with a diagonal half-hitch knotting pattern until you cover that half. Do the same with the ones on the right-hand side.

6. When this is done, take the cords in the middle (where the 2 diagonal half-hitch knots met) and make a square knot with the cords. From the first pattern you made, take the 2 cords nearest to the second pattern and another 2 cords from the second pattern too, to make it a total of 4 cords.

7. Make a square knot with the cords and repeat the same with the rest of the cords nearest to the pattern that follows. Take the remaining cord out of the 25 you cut out earlier, tie it at both ends of the wooden pole, and hang it on your doorpost. This is a detailed step-by-step method of making a nice Macramé door hanging project.

29. Circle Wall Hanging

Supplies

- 1 nail.
- 2 metallic shiny rings (1 small ring and 1 big ring).

- 17 cords.
- Scissors.
- Macramé board.

Instructions

1. Out of the seventeen cords you cut, take 16 and entwine them to the small ring using the lark's head knotting method. Take the first 4 cords from the left-hand side and make a square knot with the cords. Take the next 4 cords, do the same with them, and continue with this method until the first stage of this project is completed.
2. Going over to the second stage, leave the first 2 cords from the rear at the left-hand side and take the last 2 of the same knot, take the first 2 cords from the next knot and make a square knot with the 4 cords. Take the nearest 4 cords and continue with this pattern until the second row of the work is completed, leaving the last 2 cords at the rear, from the right-hand side just like you did with the first 2 cords.
3. For the third row, take the first 4 cords, from the left-hand side, make the same square knot with the cords and pattern the rest of this row with the same pattern, leaving no cord undone. At this point, cut out another strong rope and tie the top of the small ring to the big ring, leaving the small one inside the other one.

4. The reason for using a more durable cord is to hold the work firmly in place. When you get your work to the level where it touches the big ring, use a backward lark's head knotting method to entwine every one of your cords to the big ring.
5. Carefully and neatly cut the downside of the remaining cords to your taste. Untie the strong cord you used to tie the 2 rings and use the only cord remaining out of the 17 cord you cut earlier to tie the 2 rings. Do make sure the tying is carefully and neatly done. Tie it in such a way that it will have a space you will use to hang it. Drive the nail through the part of the wall you have chosen for the work and hang your newly-made project. Your Macramé circle wall hanging design is here!

30. Boho Wall Hanging

Supplies

- 30 big and long cords.
- 1 wooden pole.
- Scissors.
- Nail.
- Macramé board.

Instructions

1. Entwine every one of the cords to the wooden pole using the lark's head knotting method. Take the first 4 cords from the rear at the left-hand side, and make a spiral knot with them.
2. To do this spiral knotting pattern, pick out the first 4 cords and take the first from the left, over the 2 at the middle; choose the one at the right over the left one, taking the left one into space in-between the left cord itself and the 2 at the center; pull the 2 cords to tighten the knot.
3. Take the one at the left, over the 2 in the middle, take the right cord over the left one, take the left cord into space in-between the ones at the center, and pull the 2 cords. Make 4 spiral knots for each set. As you do this, you will notice that the knots you are making will be going in a spiral form.
4. Make a spiral knotting pattern with the rest of the cords. At this point, take 1 of the cords you are yet to use and place it horizontally over the current line of your cords and entwine every single cord using a backward lark's head knot. Take the first 4 cords from the left-hand side and continue with the square half-hitch knots you have been making earlier. This time, make 8 square half-hitch knots with each set (4 cords).
5. Get another unused cord and place it horizontally over the current line of your cords. Entwine the cords to the horizontally placed one just like you did with the first horizontal one. At this point, pick the first 4 cords and make a square knotting pattern with them. Pick another 4 and

repeat the pattern, until you get every one of the cords to this stage. For the next level, take the first 2 cords, and pick the nearest 4 cords after the 2 and make a square knot with the cords.

6. Carry on with this pattern until you are done with that stage; 2 cords will be remaining at the rear from the right-hand side. For the next step, leave the first 4 cords and continue with the pattern until you get to the last cords, also leaving 4 cords from the rear at the other side.

7. For the next stage, leave the first 6 cords and carry on like you have been doing, leaving the same number of cords unattended. You have to do this until you get to the middle, make the last square knot there since there is no other cord to work the square knot on. Dress the down part of the cords to your taste, make sure the cords are in order, and dress the 2 ends of the 2 cords you placed horizontally just above.

8. Get the remaining 2 cords and tie one of them to the 2 ends of the pole. Divide the remaining cord into 2 and make tassels out of them. Tie the cords you will use for the hanging of the tassels to the pole, and attach 1 tassel at each end of the cord. Drive a nail through the part of the wall you have chosen for the project and hang your work. Your Macramé boho wall hanging design is ready to grace your home!

31. Adorable Pom-Pom Tassel Wall Hanging

Supplies

- 1 wooden pole.
- Macramé board.
- Yarns of different colors, 30 cords, and 1 long cord.
- 1 small rectangular-shaped carton.

- 1 nail.
- Scissors.

Instructions

1. To start with this project, you need to make your pom-poms and tassels. To make a pom-pom, tie the yarn for work around your 4 fingers.
2. Tie it to be big, so that your pom-pom will look great. Cut another yarn and tie the rounded yarn. Tie it in such a way that the 2 sides will be equal. Using the pair of scissors, cut the 2 sides in the middle. Use the scissors to trim the work, carefully and neatly.
3. Do make sure that no part of the work is rough; straighten and trim so that the work will be nice. Trim it bit by bit, and all-round, until you get the perfect and adorable pom-pom you are looking for. Take the other yarns and do the same. Going over to the making of the tassels, take the yarn and fold it over the carton, tie the yarn from the breath upward to the one downward.
4. Cut out another yarn, tie the yarn at the top of one side of the breath. Tie the yarn just twice and in such a way that one side of it should be longer than the other side, using your pair of scissors, cut the down part of the folded yarns.
5. Make the 2 sides of the yarn come together, stretch, and arrange the yarns. Take the longer side of the yarn you tied

then and tie it around the neck of the folded yarns. Do make sure you link it carefully and neatly to give the work an aesthetic look. Now, cut out the rough part of the work (the downside) and make the tassels look good.

6. Using the same pattern, make other tassels. You have to make 15 tassels and 15 pom-poms. At this point, entwine 30 cords to the wooden pole using the double half-hitch knotting method. You may choose to make the cords to be of equal lengths or the length may vary depending on how you want it; attach the pom-poms and tassels to the cords. To make it look great, attach a tassel at the rear from the left-hand side, attach a pom-pom at the next one, a tassel following, a pom-pom, and continue in that order. Now, take the long cord that is remaining and tie it to the 2 ends of the pole. Check the pole to see if there is any cord attached to it that needs to trim. Drive the nail through the part of the wall you have chosen for the hanging, and hang your work. This is how to make an adorable Macramé pom-pom tassel wall hanging.

CHAPTER 7: Macramé Home Decors

32. Chic DIY Plant Hanger

Succulents are all the rage these days because they are just so cute and are really decorative! What is more, is that you can make a lot of them and place them around the house—that will definitely give your place a unique look!

Supplies

- Small container.
- Garden soil/potting mix.
- Succulents/miniature plants.
- ¼-inch jump ring.
- 8-yard embroidery thread or thin cord.

Instructions
1. Cut 36-inch of 8 lengths of cord. Make sure that the 18-inch are already enough to cover enough half-hitches. If not, you can always add more. Let the thread loop over the ring and then tie a wrap knot that could hold all the cords together.
2. Create a half-twist knot by tying half of a square knot and repeating it multiple times with the rest of the cord.
3. Drop ¼-inch of the cord down and repeat the step twice.
4. Arrange your planter and place it on the hanger that you have made.
5. Nail to the wall and enjoy seeing your mini-planter!

CHAPTER 8: Macramé Bracelets

33. Macramé Bracelet With Rattail Cord and Glass Beads

Supplies

- 130 cm. length of 1 mm. rattail cord.
- 1 10–12 mm. disk bead or button with a central hole (hole must be 1 mm. minimum).
- 10,6 mm. black glass spacer beads.
- 3 6 mm. patterned glass spacer beads.
- Macramé board and pins (optional).

- Ruler.
- Scissors.
- Lighter.

Instructions

1. Fold over the first 5 cm. of the shorter length of cord and lay in front of you. These are the central cords.

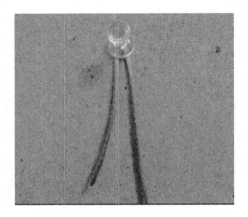

2. Fold the longer cord in half and place the center point underneath both cords.

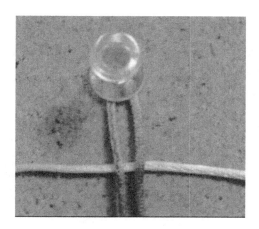

3. Starting with the left side cord tie one-half knot.

4. Tighten the knot fully and position it to create a 10 mm. loop at the end of the shorter length of cord. This loop will form

part of the bracelet's fastener and needs to be a tight fit for the disk bead to fit through. Adjust as needed to suit your bead.

5. Always starting with the left side knotting cord, continue tying half knots until you have a Sennett 3.5 cm. long. The spiral pattern can be seen forming within a few knots. Pull the first few knots tied a little tighter than normal to hold the loop created in step 1 securely. The completed section of the bracelet, including the loop, should measure approximately 4.5 cm.

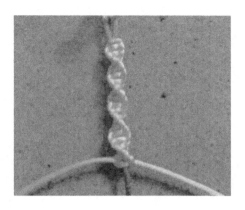

6. Thread 1 black bead, 1 patterned bead, and 1-second black bead onto the central cord and move these up to the bottom of the knots. Tie one-half knot underneath the beads to hold them in place. This knot should not be too tight. The beads should be sitting freely with the cords around them not squashed together.

7. Tie a further 4 half knots.

8. Repeat step 6, this time adding 1 white, 1 black, and then a 1-second black bead. Tie 4 more half knots.

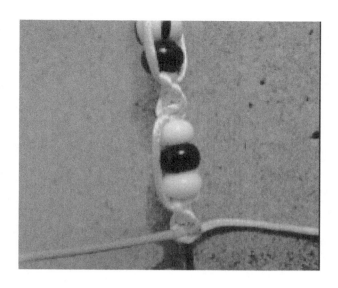

9. Repeat steps 6–8 until all the beads have been added to the bracelet.

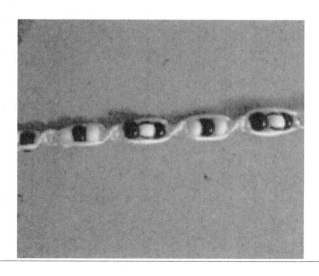

10. Continue tying half knots until you have a 3.5 cm. Sennett to match the one at the beginning of the bracelet.

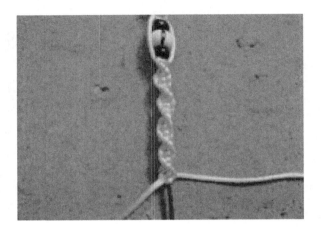

11. Cut off the excess knotting cords leaving a 3 mm. tail. Gently melt this tail using the lighter and fuse them to the final knot. The melted rattail cord can get very hot and stick to the skin so it is best to use the point of the scissors, a needle, or a similar item to carry out this step.

12. Thread the disk bead on to the central cord. Leave a gap of 3 mm. between the last knot and the bead and tie an overhand knot to secure the bead. Trim off the excess central cord and gently melt the end to prevent fraying.

34. Black and Red Macramé Bracelet

Supplies

- Red cord.
- Black cord.
- Flat bead/button.
- Scissors.

Instructions

1. Fold the shorter red cord in half and lay it flat in front of you. These are the design's central cords.
2. Fold the black cord in half and tie 1 square knot around the red central cords. This knot needs to be positioned so that it

creates a loop that the flat bead/button can pass through tightly. This forms the bracelet's fastener.
3. Fold the longer red rattail cord in half and tie 1 half knot around the red central cords underneath the black square knot.
4. Tie a further 4 half knots always starting with the same side cord so that the knots begin to form a spiral.
5. Carry the black cords over the red and tie 1 square knot underneath the half knots.
6. Pass the red cords under the black and tie 5 half knots.
7. Continue in this way until you have tied 18 cm. of knots. If you have the bracelet pinned to a board or solid surface, the bracelet will twist as the spirals form so you may find it easier to unpin and re-pin it as you work. The black cords should be flat, only the red knotting cords form the spiral.
8. Turn the bracelet over and trim away all the excess knotting cords leaving 3 mm. ends.
9. Gently melt the cord end with the lighter and press them against the knots. Heated rattail cord becomes very hot and can stick to your skin and burn so this step is safest carries out using a needle or scissors point to press on the melting cord.
10. Thread the flat bead/button onto the central cords. Push it up to the knots and leaving a 3 mm. gap tie an overhand knot

to secure the bead. Cut off any excess cord and gently melt the ends to prevent fraying.

35. Fish Bone Macramé Bracelet

Supplies
- Blue cord (divided into 2 parts, 1 long and 1 short).
- Bead/button.
- Red cord.
- Scissors.

Instructions
1. Fold the shorter blue cord in half and lay it in front of you.
2. Fold the long blue cord in half and tie 1 square knot around the shorter cord. This knot should be positioned so that the loop created is a tight fit for the bead/button to fit through.
3. Use the red cord to tie a square knot underneath the bead.
4. Place a thread on the first bead.
5. Carry the blue cords over the red and tie a square knot underneath the bead.
6. Carry the red cords over and tie a square knot underneath the blue knot.
7. Place a thread on a second bead.
8. Repeat steps 5 and 6.
9. Continue in this way until all the beads have been added.

10. Leaving a 3 mm. tail cut off the remaining knotting cord on one side. Use the lighter to melt the ends and stick them to the back of the knots. Take care with the melting cord as it gets very hot and can stick to your skin and burn. Use a needle or point of the scissors to press down the cord.
11. Repeat step 10 with the remaining cords.
12. Place a thread on the disk bead/button. Leave a 3 mm. gap between the final knot and the bead and tie an overhand knot.
13. Cut off any excess cord and melt the ends to prevent fraying.

36. Side by Side Macramé Bracelet

Supplies

- Cord
- Macramé board (optional).
- Flat bead/button.
- Beads (purple, silver, and lilac).
- Scissors.

Instructions

1. Gently heat the ends of each cord to make it easier to thread on the beads and prevent fraying. Fold 1 cord in half and secure it to your Macramé board (if using).

2. Fold a second cord in half and use it to tie 1 square knot around the cords on the Macramé board. Position this knot to create a small loop at the end of the first cord. This loop should be sized so that the flat bead/button fits through with a little pressure.
3. Fold the final length of cord in half and use it to tie 1 square knot underneath the knot tied in step 2. You should now have 6 cords, grouped in 3 sets of 2.
4. Regroup the cords into 2 sets of 3.
5. Working with 1 set of 3 cords, thread 1 bead purple, and 1 silver bead onto the outer cords.
6. Using these 2 outer cords, tie 1 square knot around the central cord below the beads.
7. Thread 2 more beads onto the outer cords and place them below the 2 already added to the bracelet. Tie 1 square knot around the central cord below the beads.
8. Repeat step 7 until all the purple and silver beads have been added to the bracelet.
9. Return to the beginning of the bracelet. Thread the cord nearest to the row of silver beads through the first silver bead.
10. Thread 1 lilac bead onto the first cord in the set of 3. This is the cord furthest from the beads.
11. Position this bead in line with the beads already added to the bracelet and tie 1 square knot beneath it.

12. Thread the cord through the second silver bead. Add 1 lilac bead to the first cord and tie 1 square knot underneath it.
13. Repeat step 12 to add the lilac beads to the bracelet.
14. Separate the cords into 3 sets of 2 again.
15. Use the 4 outer cords to tie 2 square knots around the 2 central cords.
16. Turn the bracelet over and trim off the 2 sets of outer cords, leaving a 3 mm. tail.
17. Gently melt the cord ends and fuse them to the back of the knot. Take care with this step as the melting cord is hot and can stick to your skin. The point of the scissors can be used to press it into play.
18. Thread the disk bead/button onto the remaining 2 cords. Leaving a gap of 2 mm. between the last square knot and the bead, tie an overhand knot to secure. Trim off any excess cord and gently heat the end to prevent it from fraying.

37. Cross Choker

Supplies

- Rattail cord.
- Disk bead.
- Silver foil beads.
- Cross charms.

Instructions

1. Fold over the first 1.5-inch if the shorter length of rattail cord. This will be used to create a loop as part of the bracelet's fastening.

2. Fold the longer length of the cord in half. Place the center point underneath the shorter cord and tie 1 square knot. These will be your knotting cords. This knot needs to be positioned so that it creates a loop at the end of the shorter cord that the disk bead can fit through with some pressure. If the bead slides through too easily there is a possibility that the bracelet could come unfastened.
3. Tie a further 5 square knots. Pull each knot tight as these are holding the 2 lengths of cord together.
4. Continue tying square knots until you have a Sennett 5.5-inch long.
5. Thread 1 silver foil bead on to the central cord.
6. Bring the knotting cords around the bead and tie 1 square knot.

7. Now thread on 1 cross charm and push it up to the last square knot. Because of the hole positioning, the cross will not lay flat
8. Tie another square knot around the cross top.
9. Continue with steps 5–8 until all the beads and crosses have been added.
10. Now tie another Sennett of square knots 5.5-inch long.
11. Leaving a 3 mm. tail cut of the excess knotting cords. Using the lighter gently melt the ends and press them onto the square knots.

Care needs to be taken with this step as the melted cord can get very hot and stick to the skin and burn. It is best to use a needle or scissor point to press down the cord.

12. Thread the disk bead (or button) on to the remaining cord.
13. Leaving a 3 mm. gap ties an overhand knot to secure the bead.
14. Cut off the excess cord and heat the ends gently with the lighter to seal and prevent fraying.

CHAPTER 9: Macramé Accessories

38. Yarn Twisted Necklace

Supplies

- Yarn in various colors.
- Water.
- Glue.

Instructions

1. Cut 2 to 4 pieces of yarn — it's up to you how much you want.

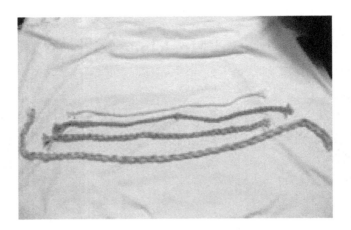

2. Start braiding, and knot using the square knot. Make sure that you secure the pieces of yarn together.

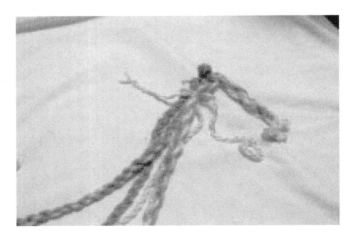

3. Knot until your desired length, then secure the piece with a mix of glue and water at the ends.

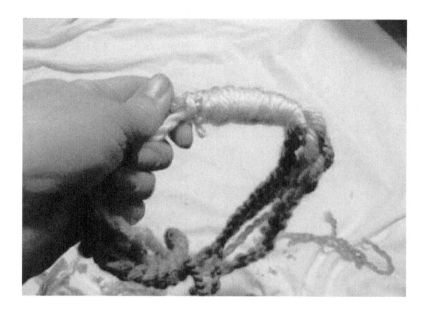

39. Filigree Lacelet Bracelet

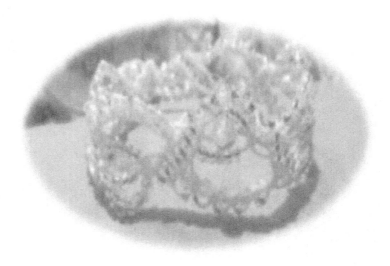

Supplies

- 66-inch length white C-Lon cord, 4 strands.
- 6 clear beads, 5 mm.
- 56 clear beads, 3 mm.
- 5 clear beads, 4 mm.
- 1 bead for a button closure, about 7 mm.
- 164 clear seed beads.
- Glue Beacon 527 multi-use.

Instructions

1. Pin this onto your project board. Tie about 9 flat knots (for 7 mm. button closure bead). Now undo the overhand knot and fold the flat knots into a horseshoe shape. Using the outer cord from each side, tie 1 flat knot.

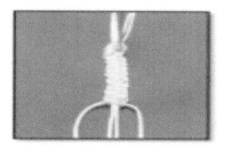

2. Take the right-most cord and place it over all others down to the left to work diagonal double half-hitch (DDHH) knots from right to left. Put 1 clear seed bead on each cord, then tie another set of diagonal double half-hitch knots from right to left.

3. Separate cords into 4 and 4. Working with left 4 cords bead as follows: on the left-most cord put 4 clear 3 mm. beads with a seed bead between each one. The next cord in line gets 5 clear seed beads. The next cord needs 1 (5 mm.) clear bead. And the last cord of this section gets 5 clear seed beads. Use the outer 2 cords to tie a flat knot around the inner cords.

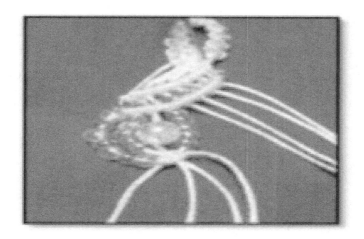

4. Working with right 4 cords: Place a 3 mm. clear bead on the center 2 cords. Place a seed bead on the right-most cord. Now use this right-most cord to tie an alternating lark's head (ALTERNATIVE LARK'S HEAD) knot around the other 3 cords. Repeat 4 times.

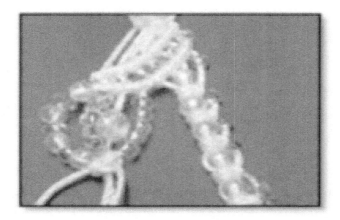

5. Using the left-most cord as a holding cord, work diagonal double half-hitch knots from left to right. Place a seed bead on each cord then work another set of diagonal double half-hitch knots (from left to right again) using the left-most cord as your holding cord.

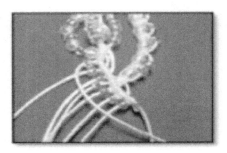

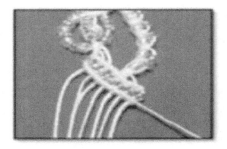

6. Separate cords into 4 and 4. Working with left 4 cords: Place a 3 mm. clear bead on the center 2 cords. Place a seed bead on the left-most cord. Now use this left-most cord to tie an ALTERNATIVE LARK'S HEAD knot around the other 3 cords. Repeat 4 times.

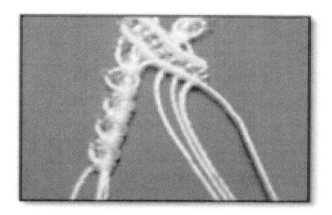

7. Working with the right 4 cords: the right-most cord gets 4 clear 3 mm. beads with a seed bead between each one. The next cord in from the right needs 5 seed beads. The next cord in line gets a 5 mm. clear bead. And the last cord of this section gets 5 seed beads. Use the outer 2 cords to tie a flat knot around the inner cords.

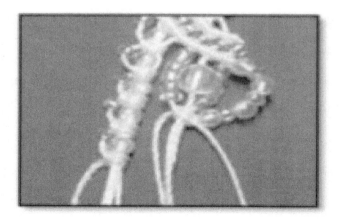

8. Repeat steps 2–7 for pattern until you have about 6 ½-inch in length.
9. Separate cords into 3, 2, and 3. On the left set of cords, place a 4 mm. bead. With the center 2 cords thread on a 3 mm. bead, a 4 mm. bead, and another 3 mm. bead. On the right, 3 cords place 3 4 mm. beads. Find the outermost cord on each side and tie a flat knot around the rest.

10. Thread your button bead onto the center 4–6 cords if possible. Use the outer cords to tie a flat knot. Glue flat knot and let dry. Trim excess cords.

40. Designer Hat

Supplies

- 4 mm. cord material (114-yard).
- Fabric glue.
- Tape measure.
- Pins and project board.

Instructions

1. For the hat created here, you will need to cut 56 cords, which should be 2-yard in length each. For a 24-inch hat cut one holding cord 36-inch long and 48 other strings, each of which must be 2-yard in length. For a 32-inch hat, you will need a total of 64 cords, 2.5-yard each. For a hat above or below these sizes, increase or decrease the size as needed (2 strings per inch). The number of cords you use should be multiples of 4. Fix the split ends of the cord with tape. It would prevent the unraveling of the strings. Tie the holding string with your workstation horizontally, and make sure it is stretched firmly. Fold in half 1 of the 2-yard strings, and place it under the holding string, so that it lies near the center.
2. Place the ends over the holding cord to complete the formed larks head knot, going downward. Move them underneath the folded line. Stiffly close.
3. Attach each end of the half-hitch knot by leading the rope over and below the holding string. It will ride over the thread you're working with when you set it down.
4. Repeat the steps from step 1 to 3, by wrapping the remaining strings to your holding string. Start working from the center and move to the ends. There must be an equivalent amount of strings in both directions.

5. For creating the edge for your Macramé hat, chose 8 cords and marked them from cord 1 to 8 from left to right. All the triangle designs are created using 8 strings, so split them out now, before you start working on the triangles. Make a square knot with the 2 and 4 strings. You only have 1 filler the string 3. Tightly firm it, so it sets against your mounted knots. Do it again with the string 5, 6, and 7. This time the filler is cord 6.

6. Now attach the other square knot under the first 2, using strings 3 and 6 (the fillers are 4 and 5). Tighten the knots firmly, so it rests over the knots above it.

7. Move cord number 1 with the left side of the 3 knots that forms a triangular shape. Lock it, so that it's tight since it is a holding string. Join the cords 2, 3, and 4 to it through the double half-hitches.

8. Move string 8 along the right edge of the triangle and fix it as well. Attach strings 5, 6, and 7 with it with a double half-hitch knot. Make sure not to attach the holding cord 1 with it, or the design will be unbalanced.

9. Make a cross using the firming strings 1 and 8, and extend all the strings in a manner so it will be easier for you to see them. Attach a square knot using cords 1, 4, 5, and 8. Use cords 8 and 1 as the fillers. Firmly tie the knots, so that the knot stays below triangle level.

10. Repeat steps 5–9, to make an additional triangle with the help of your next 8 cords. Attach a square knot from the first line, with cords 6 and 7, and 2 and 3 from the second side. Tighten it so under each triangle it meets up with the square knot.
11. Repeat steps 5–10 with the help of remaining clusters of cords. When you reach the final triangle figure for your Macramé hat, connect this triangle to the first triangle you created, to make a complete circle. Now begin turning upside down the brim of your Macramé cap. Although actually, the right side of the triangles is on the opposite side of the hat. Keep in mind that the brim which is created will be folded in a manner, so the orders are swapped. It can also be seen in the picture attached below, which is showing the rear side of the triangles at the moment, where you will be doing your work. Attach a square knot with the help of strings 2 and 3 from the first triangle that you created, with 6 and 7 from the last triangle. It is just what you have done in the previous step, and the only difference is that the cords come from each edge of the brim.

12. To create the top part, you will link a row of alternating square knots (ASK) using 4 cords per knot, 2 working cords, and 2 fillers. Starting at the place where the 2 ends were connected in phase 7 is easiest, then continuing around the entire route. To create the next row, alternate the strings. Keep the brim on the inner side while creating your hat. Mentally number each set with 4 cords. Strings 1 and 4 act as the working cords, while 2 and 3 are the filler cords. Combine 3 and 4 with 1 and 2 from the next knot over to alternate for the next lines. And the current knot lies between the 2 above.

13. Stop tying Alternating Square Knot when your Macramé hat is at least 7-inch in height which starts from the lower end of the brim, till the row of knots that you are currently working on. Keep in mind you'll cover the bottom, so you'll only have a couple more rows to add to the top.

14. Choose 12 cords that are coming from the 3 alternating square knots. Visually mark each set with 4 cords as A, B, and C. Push all the 4 strings from the set B to the inside of the Macramé hat.

15. Use cords 3 and 4 from set A (that is at the extreme left side), with strings 1 and 2 from your set C. With these 4 ropes, tie securely a Square Knot over the gap left by the strings you just put through. Tighten the knots firmly. So the top edge of your hat will appear more rounded.

16. Repeat the previous step by dropping all the remaining knots by pushing the knots inside. This will fasten the top of the Macramé hat. Do steps 3 and 4 2 more times, until you've been all the way back. Move the remaining cords into the inside until you are done.
17. Take the right side of the hat up. Note, that the front of the triangles at the top is the bottom, and while you're focusing on these final stages, they can be seen around the lower lip. Tie 2 very tight overhead knots using 2 cords at a time but from 2 different knots. Hook 1 knot, apply adhesive to the thread, then tie the knot next to the previous. Trim the excess cords after you tie the knots. As the strings are taped at the ends, you can simply cut them off to identify which cords are used. After you are done with tying all the knots, let the glue dry and cut off any extra material. Switch the designer hat's brim outwards, arrange it at the triangular tip.

CHAPTER 10: More Macramé Accessories

41. Hearty Paperclip Earrings

Now this one is really creative because it makes use of various embroidery threads and paper clips to give you earrings unlike any other. If you think paper clips are just basic school supplies, well, think again.

Supplies

- Paper clips.
- Embroidery thread.

- Earring hooks.
- Glue.
- Water.
- Paintbrush.

Instructions

1. Bend some paper clips until they resemble hearts. Take note that you may have to try a lot of times because it's expected that you may not get the effect right away. Once you have made some hearts, glue the ends to keep them secure.

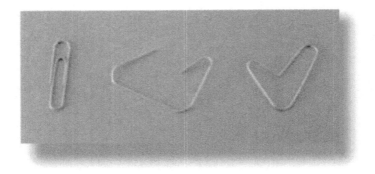

2. Wrap embroidery thread just to coat the clips, and then leave some inches of thread hanging so you could make half-hitch knots out of them.

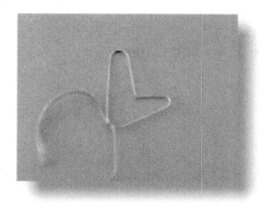

3. Tie knots until you reach the end and paint with a mix of water and glue to keep secure.

4. Let dry and then add the earring hooks.

42. Fringe Fun Earrings

These earrings could surely add a lot of fun to your ears! They're perfect reminders of festivals, or fun afternoons drinking cocktails and punch with your favorite people!

Supplies
- 56-inch of 4-ply Irish waxed linen cord.
- 2 brass headpins.
- 2 brass ear wires.
- 2 hammered brass 33 mm. metal rings.

- 22 glass 6 mm. rounds.
- Round nose pliers.
- Chain nose pliers.
- Scissors.

Instructions

1. Make eye pins out of the headpins by bending the tip and making a loophole, just like what's shown below.

2. String a glass round to form a single loop and then set it aside before cutting in half.

3. At the end of 1 cord, make a 3-inch fold and then go and knot around the brass ring.

4. Use the long end of the cord to make 2 half-hitch knots just around the ring.

5. String a glass bead so that you could form an overhead knot. Trim until you reach ⅛-inch and then make an overhand knot again. Trim once more to ⅛-inch.

6. Repeat these steps (with the exception of the first) and then attach the bead link to the brass ring.

7. Repeat all the steps to make the second earring.

43. Lantern Bracelets

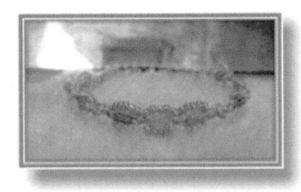

This pattern may look simple, but please don't try it if you are in a hurry. This one takes patience. Don't worry about getting your picot knots all the exact same shape. Have fun with it! The finished bracelet is 7 ¼-inch in length. If desired, add a picot knot and a spiral knot on each side of the center-piece to lengthen it. This pattern has a jump ring closure.

Supplies
- 3 strands of C-Lon cord (2 light brown and 1 medium brown) 63-inch lengths.
- Fasteners (1 jump ring, 1 spring ring, or lobster clasp).
- Glue - Beacon 527 multi-use.
- 8 small beads (about 4 mm.) amber to gold colors.
- 30 gold seed beads.

- 3 beads (about 6 mm.) amber color (mine are rectangular, but round or oval will work wonderfully also). Bead size can vary slightly. Just be sure all beads you choose will slide onto 2 cords (except seed beads).

Instructions
1. Find the center of your cord and attach it to the jump ring with a lark's head knot. Repeat with the 2 remaining strands. If you want the 2 tone effect, be sure your second color is not placed in the center, or it will only be a filler cord and you will end up with a 1 tone bracelet.

2. You now have 6 cords to work with. Think of them as numbers 1 to 6, from left to right. Move cords 1 and 6 apart from the rest. You will use these to work the spiral knot.
3. All others are filler cords. Take cord number 1 tie a spiral knot. Always begin with the left cord. Tie 7 more spirals.

Place a 4 mm. bead on the center 2 cords. Leave cords 1 and 6 alone for now and work 1 flat knot using cords 2 and 5.
4. Now put cords 2 and 5 together with the center strands. Use 1 and 6 to tie a picot flat knot. If you don't like the look of your picot knot, loosen it up and try again. Gently tug the cords into place then lock in tightly with the next spiral knot.

Notice here how I am holding the picot knot with my thumbs while pulling the cords tight with my fingers. If you look closely you may be able to see that I have a cord in each hand.

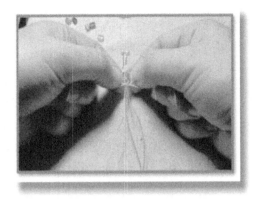

5. Tie 8 spiral knots (using left cord throughout pattern).
6. Place a 4 mm. bead on the center 2 cords. Leave cords 1 and 6 alone for now and work 1 flat knot using cords 2 and 5. Now put cords 2 and 5 together with the center strands. Use strands 1 and 6 to tie a picot flat knot.
7. Repeat steps 5 and 6 until you have 5 sets of spirals.

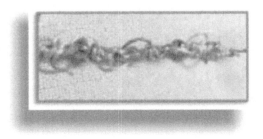

8. Next place 5 seed beads on cords 1 and 6. Put cords 3 and 4 together and string on a 6 mm. bead. Tie 1 flat knot with the outermost cords.

9. Repeat this step 2 more times.

10. Now repeat steps 5 and 6 until you have 5 sets of spirals from the center point, thread on your clasp. Tie an overhand knot with each cord and glue well. Let dry completely. As this is the weakest point in the design, I advise trimming the excess cords and gluing again. Let dry.

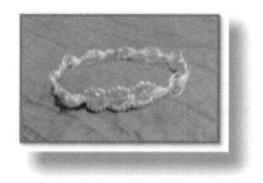

44. Hoop Earrings

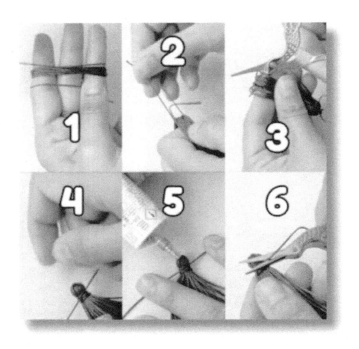

Supplies

- Contact glue
- Synthetic yarn
- Scissors.
- Jewelry caps and earring hooks to complete the ornaments.

Instructions

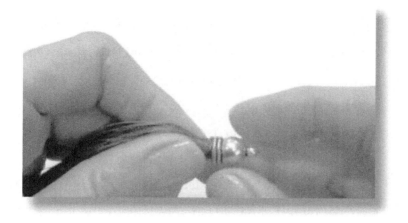

1. First of all, wrap 3 m. of thread over your fingers, hold it and tie it with more ribbon, cut the threads on the opposite end, use another piece of string and wrap it around the related part, tie it from behind and use glue to fix the knot. Finally, use scissors to cut the excess piece.

2. At this point, we should already have our 2 fringes ready to turn them into beautiful earrings. From here, we have several options; the option that we recommend is to use jewelry caps for ornaments and contact glue.
3. The last step is to use 2 earring hooks on each cap. You can use jewelry pliers if you need to open and fix the rings or any other material you use.
4. You can get all the materials used in specialized jewelry stores or by recycling old earrings that you no longer apply.

CHAPTER 11: Macramé Home Décor Projects

45. Macramé Tie-Dye Necklace

This one is knotted tightly, which gives it the effect that it is strong—but still elegant. This is a good project to craft—you would enjoy the act of making it, and wearing it, as well!

Supplies

- 1 pack laundry rope.
- Tulip One-Step Dye.
- Fabric glue.
- Candle.
- Jump rings.
- Lobster clasp.

Instructions

1. Tie the rope using crown knots.
2. After tying, place the knotted rope inside the One-Step Dye pack (you could get this in most stores) and let it sit and dry overnight.

3. Upon taking it out, leave it for a few hours and then secure the end of the knot with fabric glue mixed with a bit of water.

4. Trim the ends off and burn off the ends with wax from a candle.

5. Add jump rings to the end and secure with lobster clasp.

6. Enjoy your tie-dye necklace!

46. Macramé Wall Art

Supplies

- Large wooden beads.
- Acrylic paint.
- Painter's tape.
- Scissors.
- Paintbrush.
- Wooden dowel.
- 70-yard rope.

Instructions

1. Attach the dowel to a wall. It's best just to use removable hooks so you won't have to drill anymore.

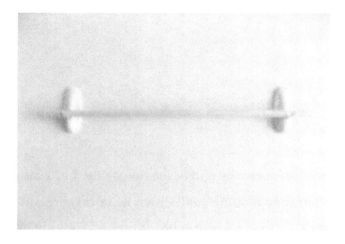

2. Cut the rope into 14 x 4 pieces, as well as 2 x 5 pieces. Use 5-yard pieces to bookend the dowel with. Continue doing this with the rest of the rope.
3. Then, start making double half-hitch knots and continue all the way through, like what's shown below.

4. Once you get to the end of the dowel, tie the knots diagonally so that they wouldn't fall down or unravel in any way. You can also add the wooden beads any way you want, so you'd get the kind of décor that you need. Make sure to tie the knots after doing so.

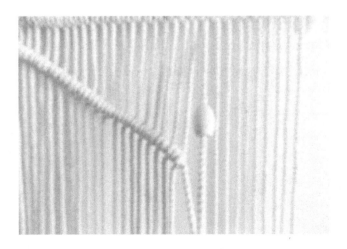

5. Use 4 ropes to make switch knots and keep the décor all the more secure. Tie around 8 of these.

6. Add a double half-hitch and then tie them diagonally once again.

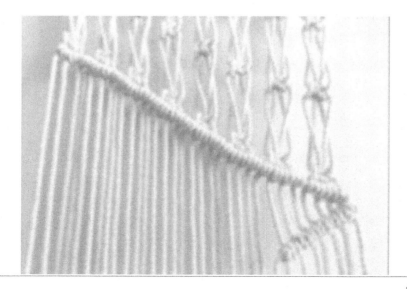

7. Add more beads and then trim the ends of the rope.

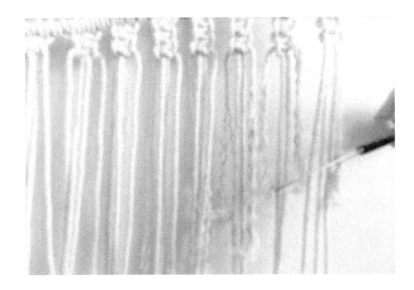

8. Once you have trimmed the rope, go ahead and add some paint to it. Summery or neon colors would be good.

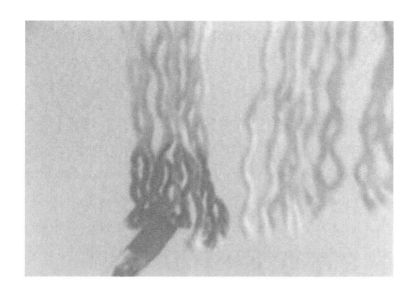

9. That's it! You now have your own Macramé Wall Art!

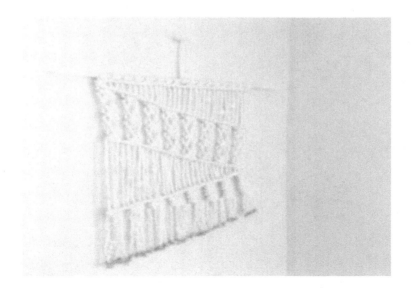

47. Easy DIY Macramé Wall Hanging

Supplies

- Cotton Macramé cord (200 feet).
- 61 m. (¾-inch circumference, 24) wooden dwell (¾, 24-inch). The wooden dowel must not be such exact measurements and use whatever scale you like in place of the wood dowel as long as all ropes are placed over it. If you want to give it an outdoor experience, you can use a branch of a tree about the same height.
- Scissors. I've been using a cotton clothesline on my Macramé string. It looks entirely natural and is quite cheap.

Instructions

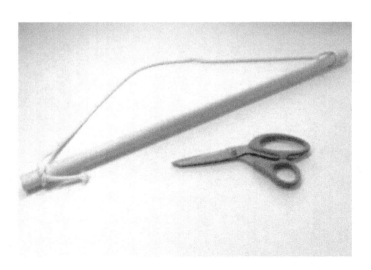

1. Cut a piece of Macramé cord that is 3 feet (1 m.) and tied it to a wooden dowel. Connect the 2 sides of the wooden dowel to each end of the thread. You are going to use this to mount your Macramé project when it is over. In the beginning, I like to attach it, so I can hang up the Macramé project when I tie knots. It is much easier to work this way than to determine it.

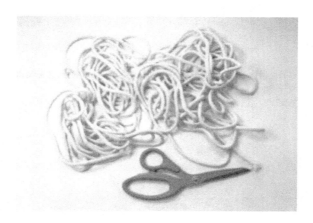

2. Cut your Macramé rope into 12 string lengths 15 feet (4.5 m.) long with a pair of scissors. It might sound like a lot of rope, but knots take up more cord than you expect. If you need it, there's no way to make the rope thicker, so you better cut it than you will.

3. Fold 1 of the Macramé cores in half on the wooden dowel and use a ladle's head knot to tie it to a wooden dowel. Join the other cords in the same way.

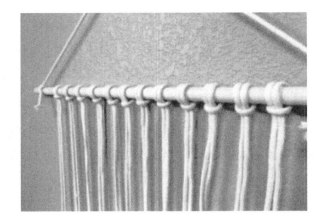

4. Take the first 4 strings and make left facing spiral stitch (also referred to as a half-knot Lynton) by tying 13 half knots.

5. Using 4 ropes to make a further spiral stitch of 13 half knots using the same pair of 4 ropes. Continue to work in 4-chord

sections. You should have a minimum of 6 spiral stitches before you finish.

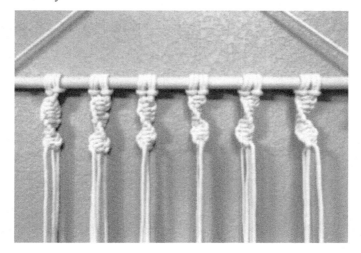

6. Scale about 2-inch down from the last knot in a spiral point. This is where your next knot, the square knot, will be found. Make a right knot profile with the first 4 strings. Continue to make the correct knots face throughout this row. Do your best to keep them all even horizontally. You're going to end up with 6 knots together.
7. **The second row of square knots:** Now is the time to start the square knots so we can have the knots "V" shape.

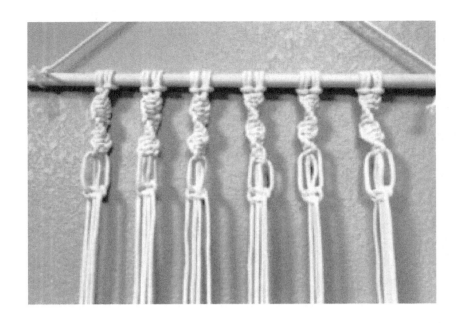

8. **Set open the first 2 strings and the last 2 strings:** Consider each group of 4 right-facing square knots. You now have a second line with the first 2 and last 2 unknotted cords and 5 square knots. It doesn't matter how you space them; just keep them for each row together.

9. **Keep decreasing the square knots:** A "V" formed from the square knots in the third row; the first 4 strings and the last 4 strings will be left out. You're going to have 4 knots together. For the fourth row at the top, leave 6 cords and at the end 6 cords. You're going to have 3 square ties. In the fifth row, in the beginning, you'll have 8 cords and at the end 8 cords. Now you're going to have 2 square ties. For the sixth and final row, 10 cords at the beginning and 10 cords at the end

are to be released. It lets you make a last square knot with 4 strings.

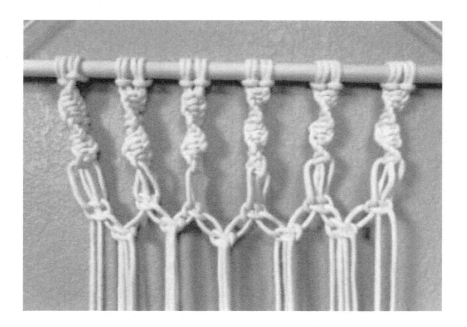

10. **Making a second "V' in square knots:** Next time we'll increase them into a triangle or an upside-down "V" For this section's first segment, bring out the first 8 and last 8 cords. That will make 2 square knots.

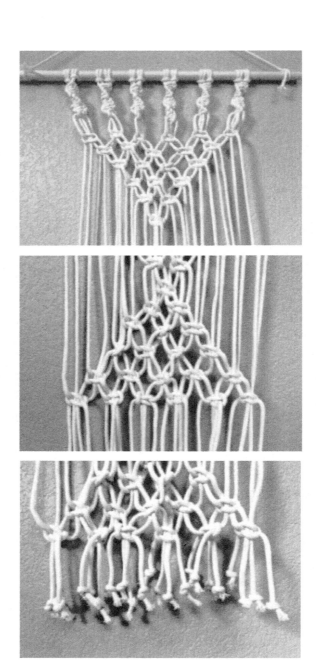

CHAPTER 12: More Macramé Projects

48. Amazing Macramé Curtain

Supplies

- Laundry rope (or any kind of rope/cord you want).
- Curtain rod.
- Scissors.
- Pins.
- Lighter.
- Tape.

Instructions

1. Tie 4 strands together and secure the top knots with pins so they could hold the structure down.

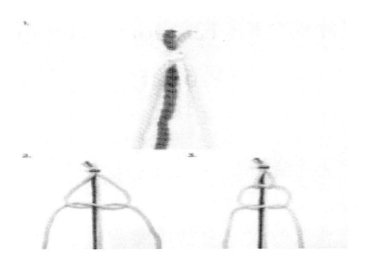

2. Take the strand on the outer right part and let it cross over to the left side by passing it through the middle. Tightly pull the strings together and reverse.

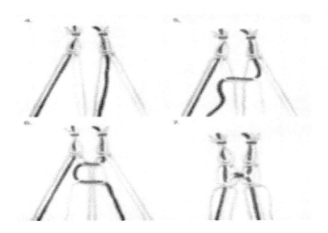

3. Repeat crossing the thread over 4 more times for the thread you now have in front of you. Take the strand on the outer

left and let it pass through the middle, and then take the right and let it cross over the left side. Repeat as needed, then divide the group of strands to the left, and also to the right. Repeat until you reach the number of rows you want.

4. You can now apply this to the ropes. Gather the number of ropes you want, 10–14 is okay, or whatever fits the rod, with good spacing. Start knotting at the top of the curtain until you reach your desired length. You can burn or tape the ends to prevent them from unraveling.
5. Braid the ropes together to give them that dreamy, beachside effect, just like what you see below.

6. That's it, you can now use your new curtain!

49. Macramé Charm and Feather Décor

Supplies

- Stick/dowel.
- Feathers and charms with holes (for you to insert the thread in).
- Embroidery/laundry rope (or any other rope or thread that you want).

Instructions

1. Cut as many pieces of rope as you want. Around 10–12 pieces are good, and then fold each in half.

2. Make sure to create a loop at each end, like the ones you see below:

3. Then, go and loop each piece of thread on the stick.

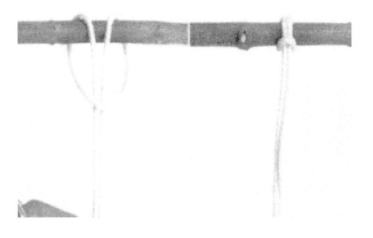

4. Make use of the square knot and make sure you have 4 strands for each knot. Let the left-most strand cross the 2 strands and then put it over the strands that you have in the middle. Tuck it under the middle 2, as well.

5. Check under the strands and let the right-most strand be tucked under the loop to the left-hand strand.

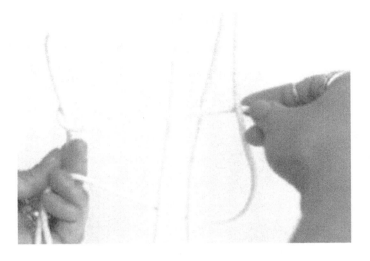

6. Tighten the loop by pulling the outer strands together and start with the left to repeat the process on the 4 strands. You will then see that a square knot has formed after tightening the loops together.

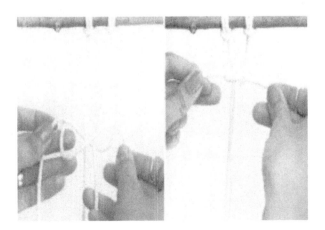

7. Connect the strands together by doing square knots with the remaining 4 pieces of rope and then repeat the previous process again from the left side.

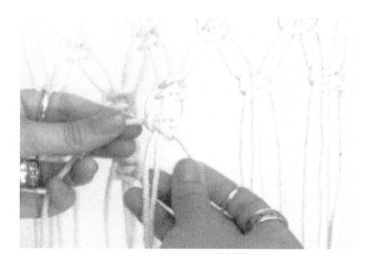

8. You can then do a figure 8 knot and then just attach charms and feathers to the end. Glue them in and burn the ends for better effect!

50. Hanging Macramé Vase

Supplies

- Masking tape.
- Tape measure or ruler.
- 30 m. thick nylon cord.
- Small round vase (with around 20 cm. diameter).

Instructions

1. Cut 8 cords measuring 3.5-yard or 3.2 m. each and set aside 1 of them. Cut a cord that measures 31.5-inch and set it aside, as well. Then, cut 1 cord that measures 55-inch.

2. Now, group 8 lengths of cord together — the ones you didn't set aside, of course, and mark the center with a piece of tape.
3. Wrap the cords by holding them down together and take around 80 cm. of it to make a tail — just like what you see below.

4. Wrap the cord around the back of the long section and make sure to keep your thumb on the tail. Then, wrap the cord around the main cord group. Make sure it is firm, but don't make it too tight. If you can make the loop bigger, that would be good, too.

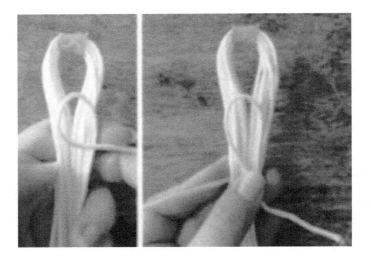

5. Do it 13 more times through the loop and go and pull the tail down so the loop could soften up. Stop letting the cords overlap by pulling them whenever necessary and then cut both ends so they would not be seen anymore.
6. Divide the cords into groups of 4 and secure the ends with tape.

7. Get the group of cords that you have not used yet and make sure to measure 11.5-inch from the beginning—or on top.
8. Do the overhand knot and get the cord on the left-hand side. Fold it over 2 of the cords and let it go under the cord on the right-hand side.
9. Fold the fourth cord and let it pass under the left-most cord then up the loop of the first cord.
10. Make sure to push it under the large knot so that it would be really firm.

11. Make more half-hitches until you form more twists. Stop when you see that you have made around 12 of them and then repeat with the rest of the cords.

12. Now, it's time to make the basket for the vase. What you have to do here is measure 9 cm. from your group of cords. Tie an overhand knot and make sure to mark with tape.

13. Let the 2 cord groups come together by laying them side by side.

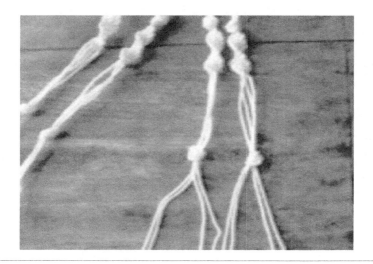

14. Tie the cords down but make sure to keep them flat. Make sure that the knots won't overlap, or else you'd have a messy project — which isn't what you'd want to happen. Use 2 cords from the left as a starting point and then bring the 2 cords on the right over the top of the loop. Loop them together under the bottom cords and then work them back up once more.

15. Now, find your original loop and thread the same cords behind them. Then, let them pass through the left-hand cords by making use of the loop once more.

16. Let the knot move once you already have it in position. It should be around 3-inch or 7.5 cm. from the overhand knots. After doing so, make sure that you flatten the cords and let them sit next to each other until you have a firm knot on top. Keep dividing and letting cords come together.

17. Next, get the cord on the left-hand side and let it go over the 2nd and 3rd cords before folding the 4th one under the first 2 cords.
18. You'd then see a square knot forming between the 2nd and 3rd cords.
19. You should then repeat the process on the right-hand side.
20. Open the cord on the right side and let it go under the left-hand cord.
21. Repeat this process thrice, then join the 4-square knots that you have made by laying them out on a table.

You'll then see that the cords have come together at the base. Now, you have to start wrapping the base by wrapping a 1.4-m. cord and wrap around 18 times.

To finish, just cut the cords the way you want. It's okay if they're not of the same length so that there'd be variety—and they'd look prettier on your wall. Make sure to tie overhand knots at the end of each of them before placing the vase inside.

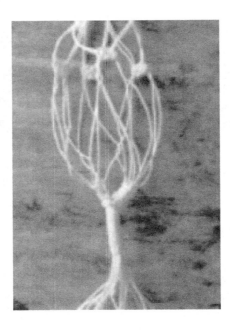

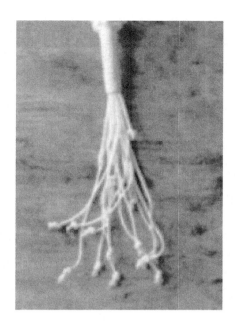

Enjoy your new hanging vase!

CHAPTER 13: Macramé Jewelry

51. Day Glow Earrings

Supplies

- 36-inch Irish-waxed linen cord.
- 3-inch 2.5 mm. crystal chain.
- 2 3-inch headpins.
- 2 large kidney ear wires.
- 2 12 mm. beads.
- Scissors.
- Cutters.
- Round nose pliers.

- Chain nose pliers.

Instructions

1. Tie an overhand knot by using 18-inch waxed linen, and make sure to leave 3-inch. Make sure it reaches 1 headpin.

2. String ceramic on both ends of the cord, then wrap the headpin with a long cord.
3. Then, tie the ends of the cords together using a square knot, and make sure to wrap the loop.

4. On top of 1 kidney wire, hold a 1 ½-inch of crystal chain. Place the rest of the waxed linen under the crystal and let it go criss-cross around the ear wire.
5. End the loop with a square knot and clean the ends by trimming them.
6. Put the beaded dangle onto the wire.

7. As for the second earring, repeat steps 2–4.
8. End the loop with a square knot and clean the ends by trimming them, as well.

52. Macramé Spiral Earrings

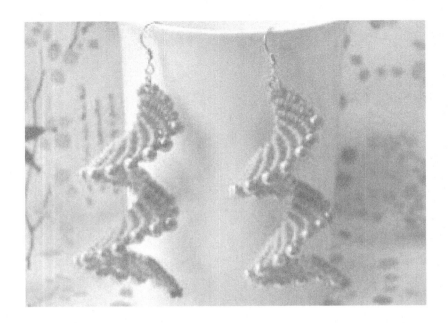

Supplies

- Lighter.
- Earring hooks.
- Jump rings.
- 4 mm. light cyan glass pearl.
- 1 mm. nylon thread.

Instructions

1. Cut 3 pieces of nylon thread at 100 cm. One of these would be the nylon thread and the rest would both be the working threads.
2. A crown knot should then be tied around the holding thread.

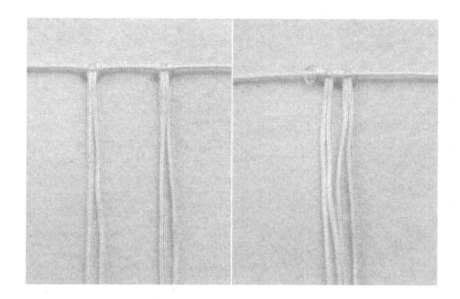

3. Check the left holding thread and make sure to add a jump ring there.

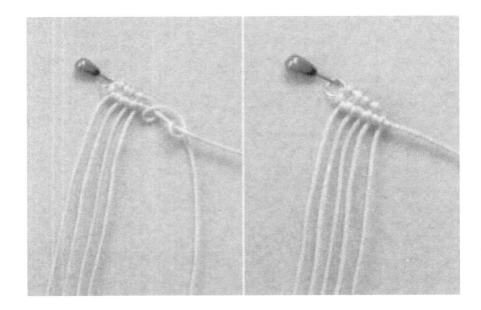

4. Over the 4 working threads, go ahead and place the left holding thread there. Use the 4 working threads to hold the thread and make a half-hitch knot on the remaining thread.
5. Tie 4 half-hitch knots on the left-most thread and then slide a pearl onto the nylon thread. Secure with a half-hitch knot.

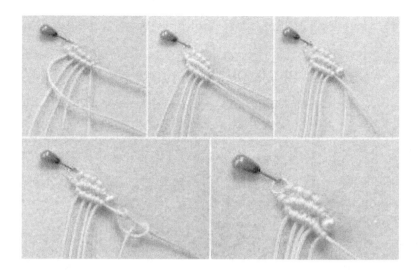

6. Repeat 25 times to create a perfect spiral.

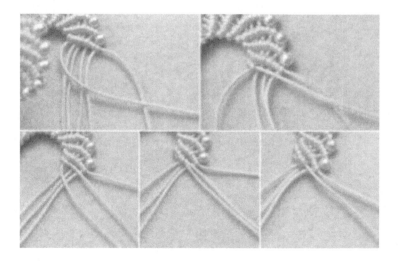

7. To fasten, get your holding thread again (the left-most thread, in this case), and let it overlap the thread you are

currently holding. Cut 1 holding thread after tying a half-hitch knot.

8. Tie 2 more half-hitch knots and slide a pearl onto the rightmost thread. Make sure to use the thread in a half-hitch again.

9. To finish, just cut some extra threads off and burn the ends with a lighter. Make sure to attach earring hooks, as well.

53. Summery Chevron Earrings

Supplies

- Ear wires.
- Small chain
- Nylon/yarn (or any cord you want).
- Wire.
- Pliers.
- Scissors.

- Hot glue gun.

Instructions

1. Fold the cord into 4, and then tie a base/square knot as you hold the 4 lengths. Once you do this, you'll notice that you have 8 pieces of cotton lengths with you. What you should do is separate them into twos, and tie a knot in each of those pairs before you start knotting with the square knot. It's like you're making a friendship bracelet!

2. Use the wire to make 2 loops out of the thread and make sure the center and sides have the same width.

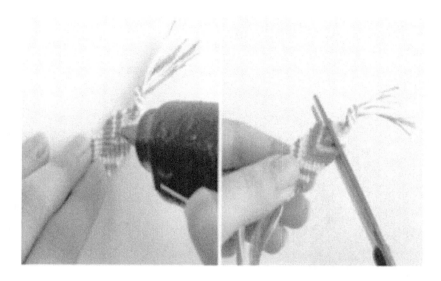

3. At the back of the bracelet, make use of hot glue to prevent knots from spooling.

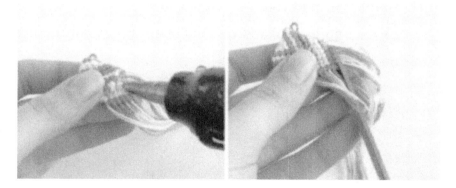

4. Fold the bracelet around the wire shortly after putting some glue and letting it cool.

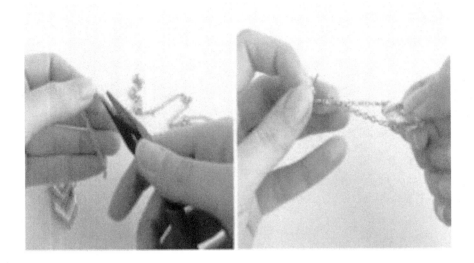

5. Use hot-glue so knots wouldn't come down again. Make sure to cut the excess thread.
6. Cut the chain to your desired length—or how you want the earrings to look like. Secure the ear wire as you find the middle of the chain.

7. Enjoy your new earrings!

54. Easy Macramé Ring

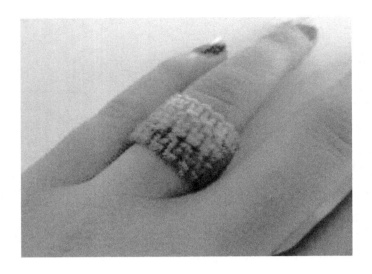

Supplies

- Glue.
- Scissors.
- About 1.20 m yarn (in multiple colors).
- Round object (just to get the size of your finger with).

Instructions

1. Wrap yarn around the round object after folding it in half. Check if it has been divided equally, and then tie the ends with 2 knots.

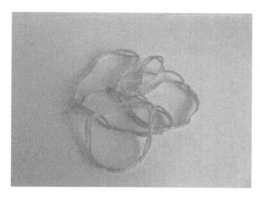

2. Put the right strand over the left strand, and then let the left strand go underneath the middle. Keep knotting until you reach your desired length.

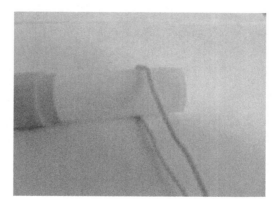

3. Pull the last knot tightly to keep it secure, and then run some glue over it to make it even tighter. Let it dry before holding it again.

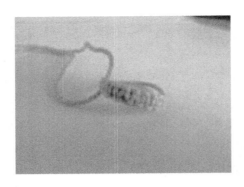

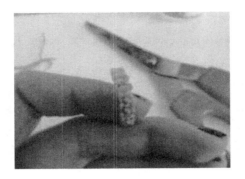

4. Wear your ring and enjoy!

55. Sun and Moon Anklet

Supplies

- 16 mm. sun/moon reversible bead.
- 2 round 8 mm. rose silver beads.
- 1 mm. 18-inch hemp.
- 1-yard hemp (your choice of color).

Instructions

1. Gather the strands together by holding them and then tie an overhand knot after leaving 1-inch of the tail.
2. Anchor the knot by slipping it into the ring. Braid around 2-inch and then make an overhand knot.
3. Arrange strands and then tie a 3-inch square knot. Slide the sun/moon bead in the area then make another square knot before adding a rose bead. Continue with 3 more square

knots and then tie an overhand knot. Do at least 2-inch of this. Go and tie an overhand knot and trim 1-inch off the ends.
4. Let the "anklet" slip off the ring.
5. Enjoy your new anklet!

56. Macramé Rhinestone Ring

Supplies

- Embroidery floss (in 4 different colors)
- Scissors
- Gemstone
- Tape

Instructions

1. Cut 3 lengths of each thread and tie all the ends together using an overhand knot. Tape down to secure. If you want to

label the threads, you could do that, too, so that you would not get confused (i.e., A, B, C, etc.)
2. Now, take the bottom left cord and cross it above the top left cord.
3. take the bottom right cord and cross it above the top right cord.

4. Take the upper left cord and cross it above the bottom left cord.
5. Take the upper right cord and cross it above the bottom right cord. Repeat the process on the other side of the cord, and then insert the rhinestone when you feel like it.

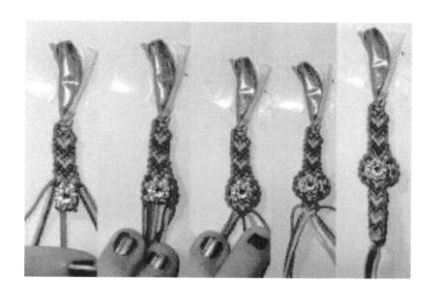

6. Pull the last parts of the cord tightly so you could keep them together.

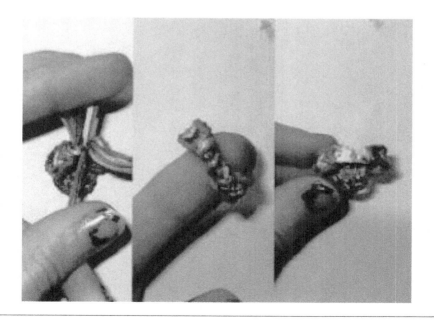

7. Repeat the process until you reach your desired length and tie ends together. Glue to secure.

57. Macramé Watch Strand

Supplies

- Jump rings.
- Closure.
- 2 mm. crimp ends (you can choose another size, depending on your preferences).
- Embroidery or craft floss.
- Watch with posts.

Instructions

1. Choose your types of floss, as well as their colors. Take at least 10 long strands for each side of the watch.

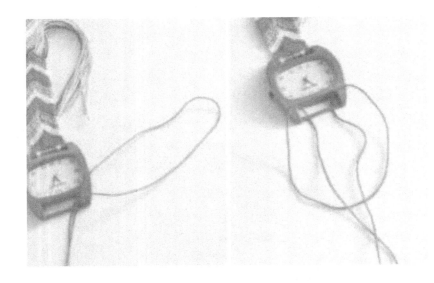

2. Lash each floss onto the bar/posts of the watch and thread like you would a regular Macramé bracelet or necklace.

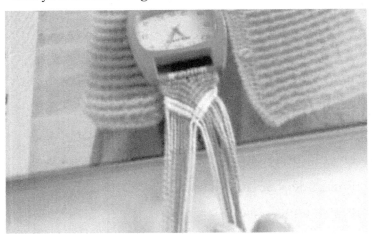

3. Braid the ends tightly if you want to make it more stylish and cut the ends. Burn with lighter to secure before placing jump rings and closure.

4. Use and enjoy!

58. Silky Purple Necklace

Supplies

- Rhinestones.
- Clasp.
- 2-inch of the chain.
- Thread and needle (in the same color scheme).
- 6-yard silk rattail cord.

Instructions

1. Cut string into 6-yard, and the other to be 36-inch. Make sure that you loop the last chain link.
2. Make use of square knots to tie the outer cord with the inner cord, and make sure to overlap on the left. Bring the string's end right under the center strings. Knot by pulling the right and left ends of the cord.

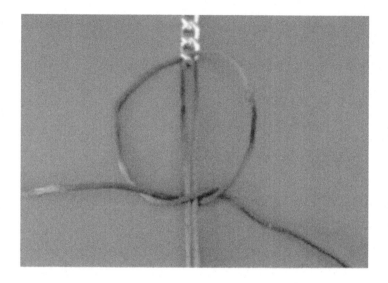

3. Repeat the process on the opposite side of the chain and make sure to pull tight through the loop and make use of square knots until you reach your desired length.

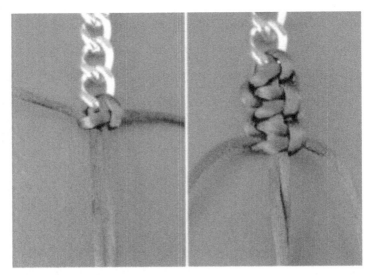

4. Double knot the cord once you reach your desired length so you could lock it up. Make use of fabric glue to secure the ends of the cord together.

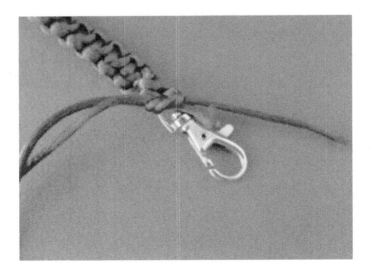

5. Attach rhinestones with glue and let dry before using.

6. Enjoy your new necklace!

59. Leathery Knotted Necklace

Supplies

- Pliers.
- Scissors.
- Chain.
- Crimp ends.
- Jumprings.
- Clasp.
- 7 silver beads.

- 5 m. of leather cord.

Instructions

1. Cut leather into 1 m. each and make 4 parts, then make a 4-strand braid out of it.

2. Make use of the square knot to secure the loops. Copy on the left side of the cord.

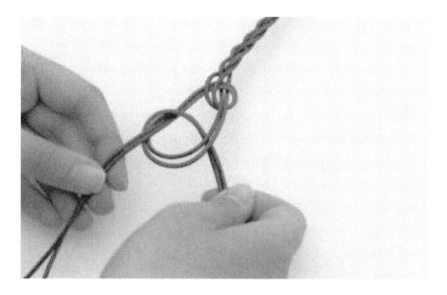

3. Add beads after you have done the first 2 knots. Hold it as you hold the right string. Create an empty knot, loop, and add some beads again.

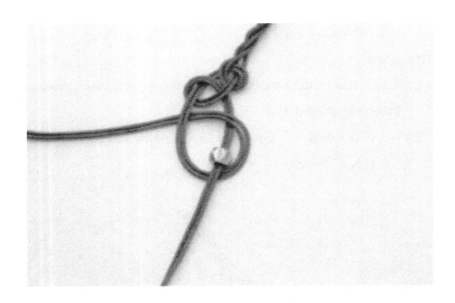

4. Secure both ends of the cord using the crimp end. You could also use glue to keep it all the more secure.

5. Attach a piece of the chain at the end with a jump ring so your necklace could be ready.

6. Enjoy your new necklace!

60. Rhinestone Macramé Bracelet

Supplies

- Lighter.
- Scissors.
- Tape.
- Embroidery needle.
- 1 small rhinestone button.
- 1 large rhinestone button.
- 3-yard 0.8 mm. Chinese knotting cord.

Instructions

1. Cut knotting cord into 80-inch and 20-inch pieces.

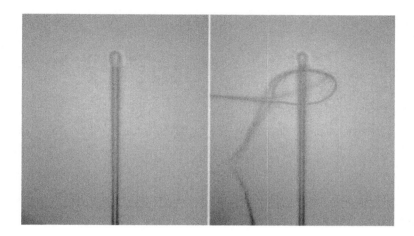

2. Then, fold the smaller cord in half and find the center of the long cord. Make sure the center of the cord is under the 2 strands in the middle, and make sure it goes under the left cord. Next, pull the cord on the left all the way to the right and middle straps so that the loop could go through to the right side. Slide the loop over the right rhinestone button.

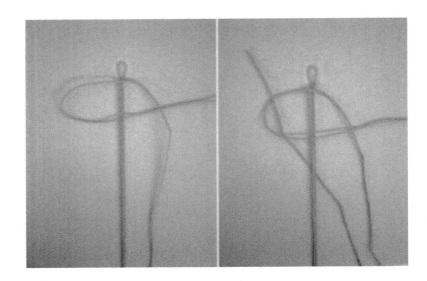

3. Make continuous square knots on the left side. Repeat the steps after pulling tightly and stop knotting when you reach your desired length.

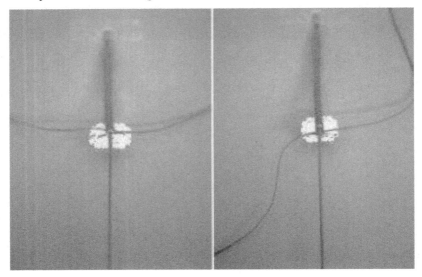

269

4. Now, get the large rhinestone button and thread it onto the 2 strands in the middle. Knot some more and add the small rhinestone button near the end, just before you close the loop.
5. Enjoy your new Macramé bracelet!

61. Intricate Lavender Macramé

Supplies

- Disposable plastic cup.
- Headpins.
- Scissors.
- Glue.
- 26 pieces 4 mm. crystal bicones.
- 28 pieces' size 6 color A seeds.
- 26 pieces' size 11 seeds.
- 4 pieces' rectangular 6 x 4 mm. glass bugles.
- 2 pieces' size 6 color B seeds.
- 1 open-ended circular memory wire.
- C-Lon Nylon cord, divided into 2: 5 ½ ft. long working cord, and 1 ft. long centerpiece cord.

Instructions

1. Use the disposable plastic cup to anchor the memory wire in. This way, you could prevent it from falling down as you work on your project.

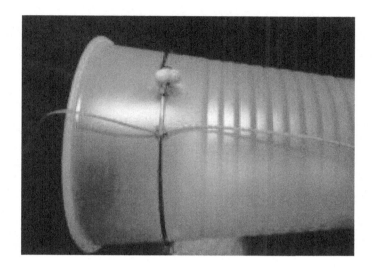

2. Pass the middle of the working cord under the wire. Go ahead and wrap a square knot around it. Now, make sure that your 2 cords are already of the same length.

3. Then, string 1 of the size 6 seeds on each cord before making 2 more square knots and tying the cord the way you tied the 6 seeds. Make sure that the knots are going in one direction and that they have uniformity.
4. Work enough sections until you reach the middle then add the final 2 beads with one square knot.

5. The new cord will now be your anchor so make sure that you tie it around the original cord. Repeat on the other side.
6. Repeat until you reach the end of the wire so you could knot 2 square knots. Slide the end cords in with a tapestry needle and then cut and glue the shortest way you can, just to keep it secure, and aesthetically good, of course. Cut the excess cords and finally tie with an overhand knot.

Conclusion

Thank you for making it to the end. Once you've mastered the simple Macramé knots, you're ready to move on to micro-Macramé and use the silky cords (more like thread) and delicate glass beads to make gorgeous jewelry. You can also use hemp to make a more natural jewelry style. You can also render your crafts using leather, silk, cotton fiber, rattail, and flax. Once you have the simple knots down, there really are endless possibilities!

The utilitarian origins of Macramé were with jute, hemp, and linen, as well as other fibers, which were mainly used for nets and cloth. As sailors and merchants collected different types of material from the lands to which they sailed, they helped to build the craft—and also to pass it on.

Fast-forward to the modern-day, where we have new technology, fabrics, and, of course, the Internet, and you have the most amazing collection of fibers, beads, and discoveries to produce just about anything you can imagine.

However, Macramé requires more than just fiber, beads, and findings. Many of the tools that you'll need to build the projects you probably already own in this book. You can quickly buy something you don't have on hand at your local bead or craft store or, in some cases, even your local hardware store.

One of the great advantages of this hobby is that with a limited investment in equipment and materials, you can get started with your craft. Unlike other wire jewelry or knitting and crocheting, Macramé jewelry projects can be easily completed on the go. You won't need rolls of wire and assorted equipment to work on your designs, with nothing more than a sturdy clipboard and some very basic supplies you can comfortably work in your lap.

Macramé is a great art and for good reasons has made a huge comeback: it's easy to know, it's cheap, and it's simple to do. You will be knotting your way to beautiful bits in no time.

Nowadays, Macramé as a hobby and ability means different things to different people. The skill is useful for many in a variety of ways. Tying the various knots will strengthen arms and hands. It can be very soothing to the mind, body, and spirit to build a Macramé project! Macramé projects call for few resources and demand materials without any chemicals or fumes; it's an earth-friendly, natural ability without a doubt.

Macramé designs range from jewelry, hangers for plants, home decorations, hangers for doors, purses, and belts. Macramé colors and texture provide a wide range of options. Materials range from various jute and hemp thicknesses to twine, woven nylon, and polyester fibers. There are not only wooden beads in projects these days, but even glass and ceramic beads are being integrated into projects as well.

Macramé has changed... Yes, it's all part of the creative cycle that endures on several levels. Both experienced Macramé artisans and experts consider it relaxing, enjoyable, imaginative, and satisfying. There are more and more options for superior Macramé to improve the decor of your house, wardrobe, and personal style for those who just want to use and enjoy the finished pieces. To decide a period of time it will take to learn how-to Macramé depends on various factors such as how easily you will learn this technique. If you have been knitting or sewing for a long time, the degree of difficulty will be slightly lower, as there are some parallels with the process.

Made in the USA
Coppell, TX
08 February 2021

49499038R00154